The
Magnificent
Book of
Vegetables

Eat a rainbow every day
with over 80 vegetarian recipes

The Magnificent Book of Vegetables

Alice Hart

OH EDITIONS

Contents

SPRING

SUMMER

AUTUMN

WINTER

INTRODUCTION

This recipe book is a proud celebration of vegetables, with their rainbows and riots of colour, arranged according to the seasons, to provide inspiration to increase your daily intake of veg in the most delicious ways. To be clear, this is not just a collection of vegetarian and vegan recipes; each one is based around a specific vegetable or vegetables and, more often than not, they are flush with wholegrains. The four recipe chapters represent this upbeat, wholefood-led way of cooking through the seasons of the year, where taste is paramount and vegetables are always fundamental. At the time of writing, it goes without saying that most of us have chosen or aspire to cut or reduce our meat, fish and dairy consumption to at least some degree. This is now a baseline norm and not a revolutionary idea. The reader's choice to eat as a vegetarian or a vegan all or some of the time is left entirely open. You will find no judgement here, only an abundance of magnificent vegetables from which to choose.

Vegetable and plant consumption is fundamental to good health and, I would argue, a colourful and delicious way to eat. I've always found the basic concept of eating vegetables to be magical, especially when you really *look* at a display of fresh produce and take in the sheer range: the colour, the tastes, the shapes, the textures. How fantastical that we can prepare and consume these beautiful, fascinating things! They are infinitely tempting, and so representative of the changing seasons. Even more astonishing that we should utilize their energy as fuel, benefitting from their vitamins, minerals, phytonutrients, fibre and the like.

Fittingly, I believe that the carrot works better than the stick. Instructing or haranguing rarely works to convince people to alter their eating or cooking habits, even in the short term, and why would it? Most know perfectly well what they 'should' be doing – it most probably includes eating a few more vegetables, most days – but practical obstacles stand in the way, from time restrictions to lack of inspiration or cookery know-how.

We all need encouragement to prioritize nourishing food in our daily eating but frankly, with all the encouragement in the world, it still isn't always possible. I wrote these recipes to inspire you through the changing seasons, with the emphasis firmly on delicious and celebratory rather than dour duty. Fresh vegetables are the worthy focus and celebration throughout this book but, nutritionally speaking, there is nothing to stop you subbing in frozen at times where it won't affect the finished article, most obviously in the case of podded peas or broad beans. Let's not be too precious. You'll notice I've generally stipulated the use of instantly available tinned pulses over pre-soaking and simmering dried ones, or I've left the choice up to you as the cook.

How can we eat 'well' every day? There's a lot of complicated, patronizing noise out there about what we *should* be doing and how we *should* be cooking. I try to ignore much of it and take a very simple line. Starting with a vegetable, or a clutch of vegetables, I build each meal around them, bearing colour, variety, seasonality, balance, flavour and wholegrains in mind. I know it sounds like a complex list of caveats, but once you get the knack of it, the veg-based meals just begin to flow. If you aim to vary the colours you eat throughout the day and across the week, being particularly generous with greens of all shades, it really is possible to get a taste for this way of eating – and to hit or exceed the famous 'five-a-day' in style. Focussing on veg is a largely economical way to cook, too, both in terms of financial cost and cost to the environment, as the emphasis is on what is plentiful at the time.

Introduction

Different styles of cooking are languages that can be learned. I elaborate further below, breaking down how to tease the most from vegetable cookery and make it your own, but you can just cook from these pages verbatim, without worrying about freestyling. A careful eye has already been cast over the satiety, macronutrient balance and, often, protein levels; the meals are intended to be highly nutritious and a delight to eat, but not lacking in energy or restrictive. They are recipes for enthusiastic cooks and eaters; no stinting or scrimping.

To keep things simpler still, I've exercised some discipline in terms of the 'chef or food writer's ego', trying to make the most of simple cooking methods and humble ingredients and spices, relatively speaking. That means avoiding those niche ingredients that could go on to fester in fridge or cupboard, first requiring internet ordering or traipsing around specialist, wholefood shops or delis. Familiar vegetables with long growing or storing seasons – such as roots, pumpkins and recognisable brassicas – are used repeatedly throughout the book, rather than dedicating recipes to scarce or exclusive varietals, such as salsify and samphire, delicious though they are.

The same applies to spices, accents and aromatics that most keen cooks would see as standard. Think cumin and coriander seeds, chillies, ginger, preserved lemons, capers, tahini, or the odd spice mix you'll almost certainly use again. All these are relatively easy to obtain. Some may perhaps contest my liberal use of pomegranate seeds and fresh turmeric – and you'll see that they are firm favourites – but they are just a few fripperies that I've allowed to slip through the net.

Being Creative with Vegetables

These are the points I bear in mind when I am cooking with vegetables in order to achieve superb, healthy, colourful eating throughout the year.

UMAMI

You'll find layers of extra umami to be an oft-repeated theme throughout the seasons here, particularly in the colder-weather recipes. This emphasis on savoury depth gives vegetarian and vegan cooking soul, whether by roasting and griddling to caramelize and concentrate flavours, or by adding umami-heavy accents such as caper, olives, sundried tomatoes, hard and salty cheeses, miso and soy. I always balance this background thump of flavour with acid and sweetness, as needed.

COOK MINDFULLY

It could well be down to an Aga-based cooking education, but I favour using the oven to do my bidding. Roasting slowly in a little fat, often whole and unskinned, will mellow and honey-baste many vegetables without the need for any effort or skill and the benefit of minimal clearing up. Compare the sweet, sonorous depth of a slow-roasted beetroot to one peeled and simmered in water, for instance. Flavours will both mellow and expand as the oven does its work. I favour a smoking-hot griddle or grill for similar reasons when time is tight or the produce requires it: maximum return on flavour and texture for minimal outlay, which is good news for barbecue aficionados. I rarely deep-fry, finding it a faff both during and after, so be assured that any deep-frying featured here is officially worth it.

TREAT VEGETABLES AS HEROES

Generally, I advise thinking of a vegetable as the centrepiece of your dish or table, keeping them whole or in handsomely sized portions where possible and constructing the rest of the dish around them. This way, you will naturally celebrate each vegetable, enhancing its textures and flavour profile as you go. You might start with spice-dusted wedges of tender, roast pumpkin, for example, as the focus of a plate. Once showered with toasted hazelnuts, draped with sweet, frazzled onions and spoonfuls of calm, fresh labneh or goat's curd, all scattered with parsley as more of a salad leaf and accompanied by tender, vinegar-dressed lentils, the scene is complete. Start with the pumpkin wedges; the rest will follow.

BALANCE FLAVOURS BUT THINK BIG

Rules are generally boring, so don't feel this has to apply in every case, but keeping a close eye on the balance and contrast of salt vs sour vs sweet vs hot will pay dividends in your vegetarian cooking. In vegetarian vegetable cooking, I like to take it one step further and make those contrasts big and bold. In practice, this means big spicing, liberal handfuls of fresh herbs, more citrus, more aromatics, more toasted nuts and seeds. This is not to overwhelm flavours, but to make the food exciting and for the vegetables to sing. Elevate

Introduction

them via the small effort of sourcing, toasting and grinding spices or adding more fresh herbs to a recipe than you might usually do.

I don't like to cloak or mask flavours with too much dairy either (and for more complex reasons to do with the current dairy industry on a mass scale), so I try to use judicious amounts of best-quality, well-sourced dairy products in the vast majority of cases. It is intended to enhance the vegetables, providing umami notes and/or contrasting temperature, texture or richness.

It is a very rare recipe that can't be easily tweaked to become vegan. I really have tried to bear that in mind when using dairy on these pages, knowing that many will need to make swaps for environmental, ethical and dietary reasons. Butter, yoghurt or crème fraîche is there for texture or flavour, when used, and carefully considered. Substitute a fabulous, grassy olive oil for butter, in most cases, and a plant-based yoghurt or cheese for the dairy equivalents.

TEXTURE IS JUST AS IMPORTANT AS FLAVOUR

This applies both to how you prepare your vegetables for cooking and eating and to how you balance their final textures with, say, toasted salty seeds, drizzles of creamy tahini, frazzled ginger strips, wafer-thin radish slices or spoonfuls of cold yoghurt. Think contrast: crunch anointed with smooth; crisp scattered over silken. To peel or not to peel golden butternut squash before roasting? Those thin skins might add valuable interest and structure if you leave them on. To finely pare raw veg into a salad or to spend the time grating or slicing bulbs or roots to make them a pleasure to eat, rather than a chore to be chomped through? You get the idea. Have consideration for the produce and the experience of eating the finished dish.

REMEMBER THE RAINBOW

Cook and eat a range of colours across each day and across the days of the week and you'll be part way there. You are very much invited to eat your greens as a key theme throughout the book. If you take on no other message, consider upping your intake of green vegetables, leafy vegetables, salads and even herbs with any recipe that *looks* green, produce-wise. It's as simple as that. There is plenty of inspiration here for cooking and eating all greens of the spectrum, though I'd emphasize the dark green kales and brassicas as the ones to really prioritize. A nudge to champion these in our daily eating is hopefully more effective when presented in recipe form.

Shopping and eating ruts can be tricky to break, but when it comes to switching the vegetables you habitually buy, consider starting with colour. So, instead of always buying yellow (bell) peppers, try yellow carrots, yellow courgettes (zucchini) and yellow dwarf beans, swapping the peppers in for red or green instead. Mix it up. Change the shopping list. Eschew those boring ruts and habits as much as you can; there's a whole, technicolour world out there beyond steamed peas and a lonely head of broccoli.

Introduction

FRUIT OR VEGETABLE?

It isn't always clear whether what you are cooking is a fruit or a vegetable – or is it? We know that a tomato is doubtless a fruit, botanically speaking, even though our typical treatment of that fruit lands it in vegetable territory. For this reason, tomatoes are treated as vegetables throughout this book. They have earned their guest status. Avocados fall in line too, as do (bell) peppers, aubergines (eggplants), green beans, corn cobs, pumpkins and squash, cucumbers, and so on.

SAVOURY STARTS

Starting the day with vegetables is an easy win. There are vast swathes of the world where this isn't a novel concept. A morning sugar high wasn't always the standard in the Western world, after all. We all respond to food differently, of course, and suggesting there will be time for proper cooking on most weekday mornings is wildly unrealistic, but I find that a savoury start sets the day up differently, so prefer to tread that path where practical.

If one eats breakfast or brunch, that meal constitutes a potential third of the day's eating and it does make me wonder how it would be regarded if we replaced a time-pressed supper with croissants and jam as a general habit. Something vegetable-based, rather than cereal- or pastry-orientated, should lead to fewer hunger pangs mid-morning and a natural gravitation towards balanced eating for the rest of the day. The tone has been set, so to speak ... and even if that tone ends up by the wayside come lunchtime or the evening, something nourishing and sustaining has been banked for the day.

There are plenty of brunch- and breakfast-friendly recipes peppered throughout this book, depending somewhat on how open-minded you are regarding suitable breakfast food and how much time there might be to spare. A green-leaf-laden, sourdough frittata, for instance, can be made quickly or the day before. Ditto an Aussie-style 'slice', slowly baked in a loaf tin and packed with spring vegetables, or a hearty and aromatic cornbread brimming with roast tomatoes and sweetcorn. They don't always have to feature eggs, either; a broth-based soup of aromatics and sweet vegetables makes a superb breakfast for more adventurous and vegan eaters. All feature within these pages and can be made ahead of time, with a little forethought.

WHY SAVOURY VEG AND NOT SWEET VEG OR FRUIT?

Vegetables, because of their lower natural sugar content and their high fibre credentials, take precedence over fruit in the hierarchy of 'healthy' things to eat. This is a book of savoury recipes – proper suppers, breakfasts, lunches and snacks – all championing vegetables, so you won't find recipes based solely around fruits. Nor will you find pudding or dessert recipes using vegetables, such as carrot cakes or beetroot brownies. Though I do sometimes use a little sugar to enhance or balance a dressing or dish, the results are always in the savoury category.

Introduction

Butter is unsalted unless a recipe directs otherwise. Do buy decent butter – fully or predominantly grass-fed – if you can.

Any recipes containing dairy have been tested using whole or full-fat versions, unless stated otherwise.

Eggs are large, unless stated otherwise. Please buy free-range if you can afford to.

Ovens run at varying temperatures and most have hot spots. A good free-standing oven thermometer will do wonders for your cooking, helping you to understand your oven's habits. These recipes have been tested in both conventional and fan ovens, always using an oven thermometer for accuracy. Temperatures given in this book are in degrees Celsius, but please remember that fan ovens run hot, so temperatures will need to be adjusted down by about 20˚C: 180˚C in a conventional oven means turning the dial on a fan oven to 160˚C.

In savoury recipes, 'salt' refers to flakes of sea salt, such as Maldon; in baking it's usually best to use fine sea salt so it is distributed evenly and subtly. 'Pepper' refers to freshly ground black peppercorns. 'Season' means adding sea salt flakes and freshly ground black pepper, to taste.

All spoon measurements are level, unless stated otherwise.

Weight vs mass/volume can be a contentious point for cooks. I use scales to weigh ingredients in grams and kilograms and have not tested these recipes using cup measurements. I cannot guarantee accuracy if they are converted into cups by means of standardized charts, especially where baking is concerned – but if you don't mind the slight risk, do go ahead and convert them if cups are your preference.

Introduction

How to Eat a Rainbow Every Day

What does a typical portion of vegetables look like? It might help to imagine a mug or cup of about 250ml capacity. This doesn't have to be too precise. Anything salad-y or leaf-y could fill that cup and then some, and be a portion. If cooked, think half to one-third of a cup as a general rule. Cooked sweetcorn, peas, beans, broccoli, pumpkin, sweet potato, chopped raw or cooked tomatoes, chopped raw cucumber and the like could generously fill the cup by half and be a portion for a typical adult. Don't overthink this; it's merely a case of getting your eye in and you're probably doing it to some extent already. Unfortunately, consuming a whole cup of, say, peas isn't assumed to constitute two portions, but a half cup of peas and a half cup of tomatoes is. Variety is definitely the key.

Thinking about vegetables in terms of their colour can be a useful tool when shopping for them and planning what to eat through the seasons. We are focused on vegetables here – plus a few vegetable interlopers that are technically fruits – but the rainbow of fruit is a similarly abundant and useful source of fibre and offers a wide range of vitamins, minerals and antioxidants. Be assured that all vegetables are high in these and beneficial to your health; I have merely touched on some of the variations in antioxidant and vitamin levels, by colour, overleaf.

If you feel yourself getting into a rut, putting the same broccoli in the trolley each time, consider swapping for something in the same colour category. And use the rainbow concept to ensure you're getting enough variety overall – more greens than any other colour, but a good mix of red, orange, yellow, purple and beige across the other produce you use. This is my interpretation of the colours and the lists are by no means exhaustive, so keep in mind there will be some crossover or discrepancy for certain vegetables or vegetable families, depending on their variety and where they are in the season.

The Colours

Green is arguably the most important colour from a nutritional point of view, so it gets triple-billing, divided into dark, bright and light colour groupings. The dark leaves are the wonderkids when it comes to nutrition and are what you should prioritize eating more of every day. Their credentials are clear: low in calories but high in beneficial antioxidants, vitamins K, A and C, folate and fibre, plus useful amounts of iron and calcium.

The sunset-coloured vegetables of the orange and yellow category are particularly high in vitamins A and C and potassium.

A purple or violet colour in a vegetable indicates the particular and beneficial presence of an antioxidant known as anthocyanin, carotenoids (which get converted into vitamin A by the body) and vitamin C.

Red vegetables (and fruits masquerading as such) are teaming with the antioxidants lycopene and anthocyanin. Lycopene can be utilized by the body more easily after cooking, so simmering or roasting tomatoes will release a powerhouse of antioxidants found to be beneficial in preventing some cancers.

The taupes, beiges and creams are pale and soothing, sometimes bitter (e.g. when blanched), but not bland if treated right. Don't be fooled by the apparent lack of colour in this grouping; its members are usually high in vitamin C and potassium.

How to Eat a Rainbow Every Day

DARK LEAFY GREENS AND SALADS

Watercress, kale, spinach, rocket (arugula), pak choi and variations, broccoli and broccoli raab, purple sprouting broccoli, flat-leaf parsley, chard, collard greens, dark green cabbages such as January King, mustard greens.

BRIGHT, SWEET GREENS AND SALADS

Peas, broad (fava) beans, edamame beans, basil, coriander (cilantro) and mint and similar, soft summer herbs, asparagus, courgettes (zucchini), artichokes, green and runner beans, mangetout (snow peas), samphire, okra, green peppers and chillies.

LIGHT AND PALE GREENS AND SALADS

Celery, fennel, spring onions (scallions), leeks, lettuce and some endive/ frisée, kohlrabi, paler green cabbages and Brussels sprouts, artichokes, flageolet beans, various sprouts and shoots, cucumber, avocado.

GREEN		YELLOW/ORANGE	PURPLE/VIOLET	RED	BEIGE/CREAM
ANTIOXIDANT		VITAMIN A	ANTHOCYANIN	LYCOPENE	VITAMIN C
VITAMINS K, A & C		VITAMIN C	CAROTENOIDS	ANTHOCYANINE	POTASSIUM
FOLATE		POTASSIUM			
FIBRE					
IRON					
CALCIUM					

PINKS AND REDS

Radishes, tomatoes, red (bell) peppers and chillies, candy beetroot (beets), red potatoes.

PURPLES, INDIGOS AND INKS

Beetroot, purple potatoes and sweet potatoes, red cabbage, aubergines (eggplant), red onions and shallots, radicchio and red chicory, purple carrots.

ORANGES AND YELLOWS

Pumpkin and squash, carrots, orange sweet potatoes, yellow and orange beetroot, sweetcorn, sweet peppers, yellow courgettes (zucchini) and patty pan squash.

TAUPE AND CREAMS

Potatoes, cauliflower, celeriac (celery root), chestnuts, white chicory, parsnips, white cabbage, onions, mushrooms, Jerusalem artichokes, white beans, chickpeas, turnips and swede (rutabaga), nuts and seeds, garlic.

How to Eat a Rainbow Every Day

SPRING

WHAT'S IN SEASON?

Asparagus

Jersey Royal potatoes

Leeks

Lettuce and salads

Nettles

Some new potatoes

Pulses (dried)

Purple sprouting broccoli

Radishes

Rocket (arugula)

Spinach

Spring onions (scallions)

Swede (rutabaga)

Watercress

Wild garlic

Spring

Spring starts slowly. It isn't an immediate riot of green shoots and abundant buds but rather a gentle warm-up, beginning in the same way that winter ends, with brassicas, alliums and stored roots. The sprouting comes later and gently, only hitting with full force as early summer makes its presence known. We need a lagging blanket of warmth and comfort in the kitchen then, holding onto soup season, leaning towards more sprightly cooking as the months progress and the radishes, Jersey Royals, asparagus and salads spring forth. Pale, deep and bright greens are everywhere.

Purple Sprouting Broccoli Paccheri

A supper to celebrate purple sprouting broccoli, but you could just as well include early asparagus, or use Tenderstem instead. At the time of writing, pine nuts are astronomically expensive; flaked (slivered) or blanched almonds would be a slightly more frugal substitute, especially as I've been generous with the quantities. I've stipulated paccheri as the pasta, but any large or giant tubular shape will hold the sauce elegantly, as would a ziti, bucatini or a tangle of fresh pappardelle ribbons. Use the excess pesto as a dip or a thick topping for chargrilled, garlicky toast to accompany soups.

SERVES 2 _____ WITH EXTRA PESTO SPARE
PREPARATION TIME _____ 10 MINUTES
COOKING TIME _____ 15 MINUTES

60g (2oz) pine nuts
3½ tbsp extra virgin olive oil, plus extra to serve
250g (9oz) purple sprouting broccoli spears, trimmed
1 garlic clove, roughly chopped
½ tsp dried chilli (hot pepper) flakes
1 small bunch of basil, plus a few extra leaves to serve
25g (1oz) vegetarian hard cheese, finely grated, plus extra to serve
180g (6¼oz) dried paccheri pasta
salt and freshly ground black pepper

Start by putting the pine nuts in a cold frying pan (skillet) with ½ tablespoon of the olive oil. Set over a medium heat and cook for 3–4 minutes, stirring often, until the pine nuts are truly golden and sizzling. Tip onto a plate and set aside.

Blanch the broccoli spears in boiling water for 4–5 minutes until tender but not waterlogged. They need to be softer than al dente to break down in the pesto, so don't be too stingy with your simmering time. Scoop out of the pan and drain well, retaining the water to cook the pasta.

Set half the broccoli aside, prioritizing pieces with good 'buds', and put the rest (preferably the stalkier pieces) in a mini food processor with the garlic, remaining olive oil, chilli flakes and basil. Season with salt and pepper and blitz to a rough paste, scraping down the sides now and then. Add the pine nuts and grated hard cheese with a splash of the broccoli cooking water. Blitz again to roughly combine.

Simmer the pasta in plenty of boiling, salted water (this can include the reserved, broccoli cooking water) for 8–9 minutes, or according to the packet instructions for your chosen pasta. It should retain a good modicum of bite once cooked.

Scoop out a mugful of the cooking water before draining the pasta in a colander and returning it to the pan with two-thirds of the pesto and a good slosh of the starchy cooking water. Shimmy around the pan to cloak the pasta with the sauce, then toss the reserved broccoli through.

Serve on warmed plates with the remaining pine nuts, a good slosh of oil and a smattering of extra cheese.

Frittata with Green Leaves

A magnificent idea for savoury, green breakfast and brunch, this time inspired by a Wild Leaves Frittata in the *River Café Cookbook Green*. There will be more greens than you ever thought could fit in the pan but fit they will. Use any combination of sliced kale, chard, mature spinach, watercress and beet leaves with accents of rocket (arugula), mint, marjoram (very sparingly), basil and fenugreek. Samphire makes a wonderful addition, but watch the salt levels elsewhere.

You could swap in cooked potatoes for the sourdough, but they won't hold and bind the frittata together in the same way. This is also very good eaten with chilli jam as-written, or when made with a finely grated, parmesan-style cheese or crumbled feta instead of the ricotta.

SERVES 3–6 .... DEPENDING ON APPETITE
PREPARATION TIME .... 20 MINUTES
COOKING TIME .... 25–30 MINUTES

175g (6oz) rustic bread, sourdough or ciabatta,
   torn into chunks
150ml (5fl oz) milk
3–4 tbsp olive oil
2 garlic cloves, finely chopped
700g (1lb 9oz) greens and soft herbs, sliced
   (see intro for ideas)
6 large eggs, lightly beaten
200g (7oz) ricotta, drained
salt and freshly ground black pepper

Preheat the oven to 220°C (425°F/gas 7). Using a large dish, soak the bread in the milk for 20 minutes to soften, stirring now and then. Crumble into small pieces (still in the dish).

Heat 1½ tablespoons of the oil in a large frying pan (skillet), about 23cm (9in) diameter, set over a medium heat. Add the garlic and greens and stir-fry for 3–4 minutes until the greens have wilted and softened. Tip into the bowl with the bread mixture and let cool for a few minutes. Add the eggs, season and mix well.

Wipe out the pan, if needed, and return to a medium-high heat. Add the remaining oil, adding the extra tablespoon if the pan is at all tricksy (a reliable non-stick probably won't need it). Now add all the egg mixture to the pan, dotting with half of the ricotta, in heaped teaspoonfuls, and quickly pressing down with a spatula or spoon to form a densely packed, level frittata. Dot with the remaining ricotta.

Cook over the heat until bubbling and golden at the edges – about 5 minutes – then transfer to the top shelf of the oven for a further 15–20 minutes until golden and set.

Remove from the oven and run a palette knife around the edge to loosen. Set aside to rest for 10 minutes. Tease out onto a board and slice into thick wedges.

Spring

NOTE
This frittata is excellent with a fresh tomato salad or eaten cold the following day.

Green Pesto Slice

This is the perfect, vegetable-packed recipe for brunch or breakfast: make-ahead, delicious, filling without being heavy … something like a frittata in essence, but more interesting. I serve it with a mixed cherry tomato salad, dressed with thyme, oil and salt, to persuade sweet breakfast die-hards that there's another path.

SERVES 8
PREPARATION TIME .... 15 MINUTES
COOKING TIME .... 1 HOUR 15 MINUTES

450g (1lb) courgettes (zucchini), coarsely grated
3 medium leeks, trimmed and sliced
400g (14oz) Swiss chard (or rainbow chard),
    stalks and leaves sliced separately
30g (1oz) butter
2 garlic cloves, crushed
a generous grating of nutmeg
150g (5oz) vegetarian hard cheese
    or extra-mature Cheddar
100g (3½oz) peas, defrosted if frozen
2 tbsp chopped chives
2 tbsp chopped basil
120g (4oz) buckwheat flour
1½ tsp baking powder
6 large eggs, lightly beaten
120g (4oz) fine asparagus spears, trimmed
2 tbsp fresh green pesto, bought or one of the
    Pesto Variations (see page 218)
salt and freshly ground black pepper

Preheat the oven to 180°C (350°F/gas 4).

Put the grated courgettes in a clean tea (dish) towel and wring out tightly to remove as much water as possible. Transfer to a large mixing bowl.

In a large frying pan (skillet), cook the leeks and the chard stalks in the butter and a pinch of salt over a low heat for 10 minutes until very soft but not coloured. Add the garlic to the pan with the shredded chard leaves and cook for 1–2 minutes. Stir in the nutmeg, then tip into the mixing bowl along with the courgettes. Add the cheese, peas, chives and basil and stir to mix, seasoning lightly with salt and pepper.

Put the flour and baking powder in a second bowl, whisking with a balloon whisk to aerate. Make a well in the middle and gradually pour in the beaten eggs, whisking all the time, to make a smooth batter. Pour into the vegetable bowl and fold together.

Transfer half of the mixture to the tin, top with one-third of the asparagus in a horizontal layer, then cover with the rest of the mixture. Spoon the pesto down the middle in a line, swirling it from side to side to marble, then top with the remaining asparagus, sitting along the length of the tin. Bake for about 1 hour until golden and risen and a skewer inserted in the middle comes out clean.

Turn out of the tin and serve hot or warm, or leave in the tin to cool.

Broad Bean and Grapefruit
Salsa for Halloumi

The prettiest of spring salsas, singing with broad (fava) beans, sweet-sour flavours and anise fennel seeds. It's one that would also work spooned over whole roast carrots, beetroot (beets) or wedges of squash, with or without the golden halloumi quota.

SERVES 4 _____ WITH SALAD ON THE SIDE
PREPARATION TIME _____ 25 MINUTES
COOKING TIME _____ 10 MINUTES

2 tsp fennel seeds
2 red grapefruit
350g (12oz) podded broad (fava) beans
½ small red onion, finely chopped
1 small bunch of mint, sliced
2 tsp clear honey
2 tbsp olive oil, plus extra for the halloumi
2 x 250g (9oz) blocks of halloumi, sliced
salt and freshly ground black pepper

TO SERVE

rocket (arugula) salad
good-quality bread

Toast the fennel seeds in a dry frying pan (skillet) set over a medium heat for 1–2 minutes until fragrant and a shade darker, but not overly browned. Crush roughly in a pestle and mortar or with the base of a sturdy jam jar on a chopping board.

Using a sharp knife, top and tail the grapefruit, then pare the skin and pith from the fruit to reveal the flesh, following the curve of the sides. Cut in between the membranes to remove the grapefruit segments. Tip these into a mixing bowl along with any collected grapefruit juice on the board.

Blanch the podded broad beans in boiling water for 2–3 minutes, then drain in a colander and refresh under cool water. Nick the dull outer skins with a sharp knife and slip out the bright green inner beans, repeating until all are double-podded. Tip into the grapefruit bowl and add the onion, mint, honey, crushed fennel seeds and 1 tablespoon of the olive oil. Season, remembering halloumi is very salty, so go easy on the salt.

Place a dry griddle or frying pan over a very high heat until smoking hot. Coat the halloumi slices with the remaining olive oil and griddle or fry for around 2 minutes on each side, maybe a little less, until well-coloured and sizzling. Transfer to a serving plate. Spoon the broad bean salsa over the sizzling halloumi and serve immediately with a rocket salad and perhaps some good-quality bread.

Spring

Jersey Royal, Spring Veg and Salsa Verde Skewers

This recipe is to celebrate the new season's Jersey Royal potatoes, purple sprouting broccoli and earliest asparagus, simultaneously pleasing poor vegans and vegetarians, who so often get a raw deal at barbecues. Consider doubling the recipe for large appetites; I've kept the serving sizes delicate, assuming there will be various salads and breads to accompany the skewers. You'll need to make the endlessly useful Salsa Verde (see page 219) or you could make a variation using a fresh pesto.

VEGAN
SERVES 4   **MAKES 8 MEDIUM SKEWERS**
PREPARATION TIME   **20 MINUTES**
COOKING TIME   **15 MINUTES**
(PLUS SALSA VERDE TIME)

1 x quantity Salsa Verde (see page 219)
300g (10½oz) small new potatoes, preferably
   Jersey Royals
250g (9oz) purple sprouting broccoli, cut into
   5cm (2in) lengths
1 bunch of asparagus spears, cut into 5cm (2in) lengths
100g (3½oz) stoned green olives
3 tbsp olive oil
salt and freshly ground black pepper

If you are using wooden skewers, soak them in cold water for at least 15 minutes, preferably a few hours, before use.

Put the potatoes in a medium saucepan with plenty of water and a large pinch of salt. Bring to the boil, then simmer for 10–12 minutes until just tender but certainly not mushy or soft. Drain in a colander, then tip into a large mixing bowl with the broccoli, asparagus and the whole olives. Season generously with black pepper and sparingly with salt. Add a tablespoon of salse verde to the bowl along with the olive oil and tumble to mix well, gently coating the vegetables in an oily dressing.

Thread the dressed vegetables onto the drained, soaked skewers, reckoning on two per person as a serving and alternating the whole potatoes and olives with the broccoli and asparagus pieces.

If you don't have a barbecue with white-hot coals to cook on, put a griddle pan over a high heat until smoking hot, or preheat the grill (broiler) to medium. If grilling, put the skewers in an oiled baking tray. Barbecue, griddle or grill the skewers for about 5–6 minutes, turning halfway, until the vegetables are sizzling, tender and charred in places.

Serve the skewers with a dish of the remaining salsa verde to spoon generously over the cooked vegetables as you eat.

Spring

Gentle Spring Tagine

If you serve this lively tagine with the cheat's version of couscous, as shown, be generous with everything you choose to plump it with (plain, dry couscous is a sad sight). I just cover dry, wholegrain couscous with hot vegetable stock, seasoning and butter (or olive oil) for richness, and leave it to swell for a few minutes. Abundant, finely chopped soft herbs, grated lemon zest, chopped smoked almonds, pomegranate seeds (arils) and slivered dried apricots are then folded through with lemon juice and extra mint leaves.

Swap the butter and honey for olive oil and maple syrup to make this vegan friendly.

SERVES 4–6

PREPARATION TIME	25 MINUTES
COOKING TIME	35 MINUTES

50g (1¾oz) butter
2 tsp cumin seeds, crushed
2 tsp coriander seeds, crushed
1 tbsp sweet paprika
1 tsp ground turmeric
40g (1½oz) fresh ginger root, finely grated
3 small young leeks, trimmed and thickly sliced
2 garlic cloves, crushed
1 cinnamon stick
300g (10½oz) flavourful, baby new potatoes, such as La Ratte, halved
650ml (23fl oz) hot vegetable stock
3 preserved lemons, each cut into 8 wedges
200g (7oz) baby carrots, scrubbed and halved, if large
400g (14oz) tin of flageolet beans or green lentils, drained
1 tbsp honey
200g (7oz) fresh, podded peas
200g (7oz) sugarsnap peas or mangetout (snow peas)
90g (3oz) large, stoned green olives
lemon juice, to season (optional)
1 small bunch of mint sprigs
1 small pomegranate, arils only
salt and freshly ground black pepper

Melt the butter in a large casserole dish (Dutch oven) set over a lowish heat. Add the spices, ginger and leeks, and cook gently for 5 minutes or so until the onions look translucent but not coloured. Stir in the garlic and cook for a minute more before adding the cinnamon, potatoes and stock. Turn up the heat to bring the stock to the boil. Once simmering, reduce the heat to medium, cover with a lid and leave to cook for 10 minutes.

Now add the preserved lemons (flesh and all), carrots and flageolet beans or lentils with the honey and cook for a further 10 minutes.

Add the peas, sugarsnaps or mangetout and green olives and simmer for a further 5 minutes.

Taste for seasoning, adding salt and pepper as needed (you can add a little lemon juice here if it needs perking up, but the preserved lemon wedges should have covered that job). Remove from the heat and serve showered with mint sprigs and pomegranate arils, on a bed of the tarted-up couscous, as described in the intro.

Green Quinoa Breakfast Bowls

The title contains the word breakfast, which means weekend, I think, unless you have a lot of time on your hands in the mornings. It's a reminder that vegetables are perfectly suitable for eating at the beginning of the day, especially green ones, served with harissa dressings, poached eggs and yoghurt. This would make an equally good light lunch or supper.

SERVES 4

PREPARATION TIME .... 10 MINUTES
COOKING TIME .... 25–35 MINUTES

150g (5oz) quinoa
4 spring onions (scallions), white and green parts
    finely sliced separately
300ml (10fl oz) fresh vegetable stock
100g (3½oz) pack of coriander (cilantro), a few
    sprigs reserved, the rest roughly chopped
1 heaped tbsp harissa paste
1 tsp honey
2 lemons
2 garlic cloves, crushed
1½ tsp ras el hanout spice mix
2 tbsp olive oil
4 baby romesco broccoli heads (or use equivalent
    standard broccoli), sliced vertically into
    2cm (¾in) thick steaks
4 very fresh eggs
150g (5oz) Greek yoghurt
salt and freshly ground black pepper

TO SERVE

warmed flatbreads

NOTE

If your eggs are fresh enough, they will hold without the need for any swirls or vinegar tomfoolery.

Start with the green quinoa. Put a large frying pan (skillet) over a medium heat. Add the quinoa and toss around the pan for 3–4 minutes until a shade or two darker and smelling nutty. Add the white spring onions and the stock and bring to the boil, then cover with a lid and simmer for 15 minutes until the grains have unfurled and no liquid remains.

Blitz the roughly chopped coriander in a mini food processor until very finely chopped (or do this by hand). Add half to the quinoa and stir through. Put the other half in a bowl with the harissa and honey. Cut 1 lemon into wedges and set aside. Finely grate the zest of the other lemon and squeeze the juice and add to the mixture to make the dressing. Season to taste.

To cook the broccoli, combine the garlic, ras el hanout and oil, seasoning with salt and pepper, then brush the broccoli slices with the spiced oil. Place a large frying pan over a high heat until smoking hot. Lay the broccoli slices out in the pan in a single layer and place a heavy pan (or similar) on top to weigh them down. Cook for 2–3 minutes until slightly charred, then flip them over and repeat. Repeat this process as many times as necessary to cook all the broccoli, keeping the cooked slices covered loosely with kitchen foil on a plate.

To poach the eggs, half-fill a deep-sided frying pan or sauté pan with water and bring up to the gentlest, fizzing boil – barely a blip really. Carefully crack each egg into a small mug, then slide into the water as gently as possible. Poach gently for 3–4 minutes, depending on whether you like the yolks to be runny or partly set. Remove with a slotted spoon to drain on paper towel.

Serve the broccoli, yoghurt and eggs on the green quinoa in shallow bowls, spooning the dressing over and accompanying with extra coriander sprigs and the reserved lemon wedges. Scatter with the finely sliced spring onion tops and tuck warmed flatbreads in at the side.

Spring

Green Pad Thai

This is based on a classic pad Thai (without the fish sauce, of course), but with plenty of omelette, peanuts and a heavy hand with the greens to give it real character to accompany its vegan credentials. It makes a brilliant supper for two – that way, you can keep the wok or pan hot enough to stir-fry properly without steaming or braising the noodles – and is a cinch to throw together once you've prepped all the components.

VEGAN
SERVES 2
PREPARATION TIME _____ 30 MINUTES
COOKING TIME _____ 20 MINUTES

100g (3½oz) flat, brown rice noodles
50g (1¾oz) unsalted peanuts
4 tbsp tamarind purée
4 tbsp vegetarian fish sauce
1½–2 tbsp palm sugar or soft brown sugar, to taste
½ tsp hot chilli powder
3 tbsp groundnut (peanut) oil
300g (10½oz) sliced greens, such as pak choy (bok choi), choy sum, chard, kale, cavolo nero, mustard greens or mature spinach leaves
2 garlic cloves, finely chopped
3 large eggs
100g (2½oz) beansprouts
2 tbsp chopped Chinese or garlic chives, or green spring onion (scallion) tops

TO SERVE
1 red chilli, finely sliced
lime wedges
chilli sauce (optional)

First, soak the rice noodles in plenty of lukewarm water for 20 minutes. This is to soften them just enough to be pliable, not to cook them.

Meanwhile, preheat the oven to 190°C (375°F/gas 5), spread the peanuts out on a baking tray and roast for about 7 minutes, shaking the tray halfway through until golden. Cool, then crush or chop quite finely.

Put the tamarind purée, vegetarian fish sauce and 1 tablespoon of the sugar in a small saucepan with 1 tablespoon of water. Heat through gently for 5 minutes, then add the chilli powder. Taste and stir in the remaining palm sugar, if you wish. There should be a good balance of salty, sour, sweet and hot flavours.

Drain the noodles very thoroughly. Have the tamarind sauce on hand, along with all the remaining prepared ingredients and a small dish of water.

Set a wok over a high heat and add 2 tablespoons of the groundnut oil. Once smoking hot, throw in the greens and stir-fry for 1–2 minutes until they start to soften (this will depend somewhat on the type of greens used). Add the garlic and cook for a minute more. Add half the tamarind sauce and tip the noodles into the wok. Stir-fry until the noodles just soften, adding a splash of water if they stick. Taste and add some or all of the remaining sauce, as needed.

Push the noodles to the side of the wok and add the remaining oil. Crack the eggs into the base, stirring to scramble before letting them set into a makeshift omelette. Tumble the noodles and egg together, throwing half of the peanuts, the beansprouts and the garlic chives or spring onion greens into the wok at the same time. Toss through until the beansprouts turn translucent, then serve the noodles with the remaining peanuts and sliced chilli on top. Add lime wedges on the side and offer chilli sauce, if liked.

Summer Rolls in Spring

The picture shows a version of the Vegan Nuoc Cham sauce (see page 219) for dipping the summer rolls, but the silken, satay-style cashew sauce in the recipe for Spicy Tofu-Cashew Satay Bowls with Grilled Asparagus and Edamame (see page 110) is a highly recommended addition. Vary the summer roll filling ingredients as you wish. I've kept these very light, green and salad-y for spring as a blueprint and a vehicle for raw vegetables, but marinated tofu, cooked vermicelli noodles, slices of avocado, griddled asparagus and roast spears of sweet potato all make very welcome enhancements.

VEGAN
SERVES 4 AS A SNACK OR LIGHT STARTER
PREPARATION TIME 40 MINUTES
COOKING TIME 5 MINUTES

1 x quantity Vegan Nuoc Cham (see page 219), finishing with the 1–2 finely chopped green bird's eye chillies
12 medium-sized rice paper wrappers
120g (4oz) beansprouts
½ large cucumber, deseeded and sliced into matchsticks
4 spring onions (scallions), cut into 6cm (2½in) lengths and finely shredded
24 sugarsnap peas, halved lengthways
1 handful of pea shoots
1 handful of Thai basil leaves
1 handful of mint leaves
1 handful of coriander (cilantro) leaves

TO SERVE

60g (2oz) peanuts or cashews, toasted and crushed (optional)
12 iceberg lettuce leaves (optional)

Make the dipping sauce as per the recipe on page 219, adding the 1–2 finely chopped, green bird's eye chillies, according to your preference for heat, to finish the sauce.

Put the sauce and the optional crushed nuts in little pots ready to serve alongside the summer rolls, for dipping as you eat.

To make the summer rolls, dip each rice paper wrapper in a bowl of lukewarm water for a few seconds until it just loses its friable texture and begins to soften. Shake dry, then lay them on a damp tea (dish) towel, spread taut over a chopping board. This will make it easier to roll the wrappers without them sticking.

Neatly arrange one-twelfth of the filling ingredients on a wrapper in a pile at the end closest to you, leaving a 2–3cm (1 in) border clear at the edges either side. Try to make sure the herbs look pretty against the transparent wrapper, dotting a couple further up the circle so they will show through once the rolling starts, but don't worry too much – this is a fiddly business and takes practice. Fold in the sides of the wrapper and roll up, working away from you as gently but firmly as you can, and starting from the filling end to make a cylinder with folded-in ends. Repeat with the other eleven rice paper wrappers.

For extra crunch, wrap each roll in an iceberg lettuce leaf to eat, if liked, then serve straight away.

Smashed New Potato Salad with Blue Cheese and Chicory

Delicious upon delicious – if you like crisp-edged, hot, smashed potatoes, melting blue cheese, the crunch of chicory (endive) and radish and a sweet mustard dressing, that is.

SERVES 4
PREPARATION TIME .... 25 MINUTES
COOKING TIME .... 40 MINUTES

500g (1lb 2oz) baby new potatoes, scrubbed
6 tbsp extra virgin olive oil
2 tsp finely chopped rosemary leaves
150g (5oz) blue cheese, such as Stilton, crumbled
1 heaped tsp wholegrain mustard
juice of 1 lemon
2 tsp honey
3 small heads of chicory (endive), bases trimmed
    and leaves separated
100g (3½oz) radishes, very finely sliced
4 spring onions (scallions), finely sliced or shredded
2 tbsp finely chopped chives
salt and freshly ground black pepper

Preheat the oven to 200°C (400°F/gas 6).

Simmer the new potatoes in plenty of salted, boiling water for 15 minutes. Drain well, then tip into a large roasting pan and gently crush or flatten them with the base of a sturdy jar. Drizzle with 2 tablespoons of the oil, season well, especially with black pepper, and scatter with rosemary. Roast for 15 minutes, then strew with half of the crumbled cheese and return to the oven for 10 minutes more until the cheese is bubbling and the potatoes are golden.

Meanwhile, combine the remaining 4 tablespoons of oil with the mustard, lemon juice, honey and seasoning to taste. Gently toss the chicory leaves and sliced radish with the dressing, smashed potatoes, remaining cheese, spring onions and chives on a platter. Serve while the potatoes are still warm.

Spring

Shaved Asparagus, Beetroot, Fennel and Wild Rice Salad with a Sweet Mustard Dressing

Tender and new spring vegetables are carefully sliced – dust off your mandolines and sharp peelers – but kept raw in this colourful salad. Asparagus doesn't always have to be steamed or roasted, after all. The same goes for beets. The key lies in slicing them finely enough. A maple and mustard dressing brings everything together, and isn't at all cloying when paired with so much crisp, fresh texture and chewy, sweet hazelnut-scented wild rice.

Note that to shorten the wild rice cooking time, you can put it in a heatproof bowl the evening beforehand and cover generously with boiling water. Leave to soak for 12 hours overnight. Drain and cook as below, but using only 300ml (10fl oz) of water and simmering for 20 minutes until tender.

VEGAN

SERVES 2	AS A MAIN OR 4 AS A SIDE
PREPARATION TIME	30 MINUTES
COOKING TIME	1 HOUR

120g (4oz) wild rice
1 fennel bulb, trimmed and any fronds reserved
1 handful of ice cubes
3 small beetroot (beets), preferably in a mix
    of colours such as candy and red
150g (5oz) asparagus spears, bases trimmed
100g (3½oz) radishes, very finely sliced
salt and freshly ground black pepper
½ punnet mustard cress, snipped

FOR THE DRESSING

2 tsp maple syrup
½ small red onion, very finely chopped
½ small garlic clove, crushed
1 tsp finely chopped dill
finely grated zest and juice of 1 large lemon
4½ tbsp extra virgin olive oil
1 tbsp Dijon mustard

Put the rice in a medium saucepan and add 450ml (15¾fl oz) of water. Bring to the boil, add a pinch of salt and partially cover with a lid. Simmer for 45 minutes until the water has been absorbed. The black grains should be just tender and beginning to burst open, revealing their paler insides. Set aside with the lid on for 15 minutes or so – it will continue to cook through.

Meanwhile, prepare all the shaved vegetables, ideally using a mandoline but, failing that, a very sharp knife and a swivel vegetable peeler.

Halve the fennel bulb, trim any tough root section away and slice as thinly as possible. Transfer to a large bowl and cover with cold water and a handful of ice cubes to shock the fennel slices, making them crisp and curl up. Chop the fennel fronds and set aside.

Peel away the beetroot skins and slice the beets paper-thin. Use the vegetable peeler to carefully pare the asparagus spears into long, fine slices, from base to tip.

To make the dressing, combine the maple syrup and 2 tablespoons of water with the red onion, garlic, dill, lemon zest and juice, extra virgin olive oil and Dijon mustard. Season to taste.

Drain the fennel in a colander and pat dry in a clean tea (dish) towel. Toss all the prepared vegetables together in a large mixing bowl, then add the warm rice and half of the dressing, tumbling through to mix.

Divide the salad between two large or four small serving plates, scattering with snipped cress and drizzling with the remaining dressing.

Baby Beets with Yoghurt and Herbs

Any beetroot colour will do in this prettiest and simplest of spring starters; it doesn't matter much if you can't find the candy-striped varieties. Small beetroots are sweetest and best at this time of year, but if you do use larger, older ones, cook four of them for an hour or so, as below, before slicing into wedges.

SERVES 4 .... AS A STARTER
PREPARATION TIME .... 10 MINUTES
COOKING TIME .... 50 MINUTES

12 small, candy-coloured beetroot (beet)
    of various hues, scrubbed, and any tender,
    young leaves reserved
2 garlic cloves
4 tbsp extra virgin olive oil, plus extra for drizzling
4 tbsp red wine vinegar
6 lemon thyme sprigs, plus extra leaves to serve
a small handful of spring herb and salad leaves,
    such as dill, mint, pea shoots and thyme
300g (10½oz) goat's milk Greek yoghurt
    (or standard Greek yoghurt)
salt and freshly ground black pepper

Preheat the oven to 190°C (375°F/gas 5).

Put the beets in the middle of a large square of foil with the garlic cloves. Bring the foil up slightly to create a bowl and drizzle with 2 tablespoons of the olive oil, half the vinegar and 2 tablespoons of water. Tuck the thyme sprigs in, scrunching the edges of the foil together to form a loose, but tightly sealed parcel. Place on a baking tray and cook for about 50 minutes until the beets are tender to the point of a knife.

Open, being careful not to lose any pink-red liquid sitting in the package. Strain the liquid into a small bowl and add the roast garlic, crushing it into the dressing. Stir in the remaining 2 tablespoons each of olive oil and vinegar, taste and adjust the seasoning, as needed. It should be delightfully pink.

Gently rub or pare the skins away from the roast beets, halving or quartering them according to size.

Stir a good pinch of salt into the yoghurt to season and divide between small serving bowls. Spoon the warm, candy beets over the tender herb or salad leaves and any reserved, young beet leaves. Spoon the garish vinegar dressing over to finish, with an extra drizzle of good olive oil.

Spring

Roast Rainbow Carrots
with Olives, Spelt and Tarragon

A rainbow of new-season, roast baby carrots with a tarragon, spelt and olive tabbouleh of sorts, spiked through with chilli, orange zest and a citrus-olive oil dressing. This is more of a side, to be eaten with good, spring things, such as goat's curd and perhaps some roast asparagus or newest broad (fava) beans, but you could certainly eat it as a relaxed main course for two, or double up on the spelt quantities to make it more substantial.

SERVES 4	AS A SIDE
PREPARATION TIME	20 MINUTES
COOKING TIME	45 MINUTES

450g (1lb) baby rainbow carrots, scrubbed
6 tbsp extra virgin olive oil
2 banana or echalion shallots, halved and finely chopped
2 garlic cloves, finely chopped
150g (5oz) pearled spelt
grated zest and juice of 1 small orange
1½ tbsp sherry vinegar
1 tsp honey or maple syrup
1 pinch of dried chilli (hot pepper) flakes
90g (3oz) kalamata olives, stoned and roughly sliced
1 handful of carrot tops, chervil or flat-leaf parsley, finely chopped
1 small bunch of tarragon, roughly chopped
salt and freshly ground black pepper

Preheat the oven to 200°C (400°F/gas 6).

Toss the carrots with 1½ tablespoons of the olive oil, season well with salt and pepper, then spread them out in a roasting pan. Roast for 30–35 minutes, shaking them around halfway through, until sizzling, caramelized and tender.

Meanwhile, put another 1½ tablespoons of oil in a medium saucepan set over a low-medium heat. Add the shallots with a pinch of salt and cook, stirring, for about 7 minutes until beginning to soften. Add the garlic and cook for a further minute or so, followed by the spelt grains, turning to coat in the oil. Add 400ml (13fl oz) of water, bring to the boil, cover with a lid and simmer gently for about 35 minutes until the grains are tender and the water has been absorbed. Set aside with the lid on.

Combine the remaining 3 tablespoons of olive oil with the orange zest and juice, the sherry vinegar, honey and chilli flakes to make a light dressing.

Fold the olives, chopped carrot tops or herbs and nearly all the chopped tarragon through the spelt. Spoon this mixture over the carrots, still in their roasting pan or on a separate serving platter, then spoon the orange dressing over to finish. Scatter with the remaining tarragon leaves and serve warm or cool.

Spring

What would a vegetarian book in celebration of vegetables be without a vegan kale salad recipe? Massaging the dressing into the kale and setting it aside for a few minutes will make a big difference to the raw leaves, tenderizing them. Repurpose the dressing here as a dip for raw carrots and fennel or as a dressing for all manner of shredded slaws.

VEGAN
SERVES 2–3
PREPARATION TIME _____ 30 MINUTES

FOR THE SALAD

2 small shallots, very finely sliced into rounds
1 large pinch of salt
300g (10½oz) cavolo nero or similar kale leaves, tough stalks removed and leaves shredded
2 crisp eating (dessert) apples, cored, if liked, and sliced into paper-thin rounds
200g (7oz) Taifun smoked tofu with almonds and sesame seeds, or similar firm tofu, sliced
1 tbsp toasted sesame seeds

FOR THE DRESSING

20g (¾oz) fresh ginger root, peeled and roughly chopped
1 garlic clove, roughly chopped
juice of 1 large lemon
2½ tbsp toasted sesame oil
1 tbsp well-stirred light tahini
1 tbsp maple syrup or date molasses
salt and freshly ground black pepper

Start by soaking the sliced shallots in a bowl of cold water with a pinch of salt for 10 minutes to remove their bite. Drain and pat dry.

To make the dressing, put all the ingredients in a blender or mini food processor with 4 tablespoons of warm water. Blend until smooth, then check the seasoning, adding more salt and pepper if needed.

Put the kale in a mixing bowl and add half of the dressing, firmly massaging it into the leaves with clean hands. Do this for a minute or two, then set aside to tenderize for 5 minutes.

Tumble the apple, tofu, shallots and sesame seeds through the kale, divide between serving plates and spoon the remaining dressing over the top to serve.

Spring

Rainbow-Layered Salad Bagel

More of an idea than a recipe, gently encouraging an old-fashioned salad sandwich in rainbow-coloured-bagel guise. If you make no other part of it, try the avocado, basil and goat's cheese cream. It's superb in and on so many wraps, sandwiches and toasts – especially useful for mayonnaise haters craving a sauce-y sandwich.

MAKES 2
PREPARATION TIME 15 MINUTES

2 carrots, scrubbed and coarsely grated
1 beetroot (beet), scrubbed and sliced paper-thin
50g (1¾oz) radish, preferably a large one, sliced
    paper-thin
2 tbsp lemon juice
1 large, very ripe avocado, halved and stoned
1 tbsp finely chopped basil, plus extra leaves
    to serve
100g (3½oz) soft goat's cheese
2 wholegrain, multi-seed bagels, split horizontally
1 small handful of alfalfa sprouts
1 small handful of mixed sprouts or microgreens,
    such as purple radish, sunflower, basil or chard
salt and freshly ground black pepper

Put the grated carrot, and sliced beetroot and radish in separate bowls or just piles on a chopping board, tossing each one with a teaspoon of lemon juice.

Make the avocado cream by scooping the very ripe avocado into a bowl with the remaining tablespoon of lemon juice, black pepper and a pinch of salt. Whip with a fork until smooth, then beat in the basil and soft goat's cheese to make a pale green, herb-flecked cream.

Lightly toast the bagels (in a griddle pan set over a high heat if you don't have a toaster), then spread all the cut sides generously with the avocado cream, avoiding the central void. Layer the base half up with alfalfa sprouts, grated carrot, radish slices, beetroot slices, mixed sprouts and a couple of extra basil leaves, carefully finishing with the avocado cream-laden bagel top, pressed down gently. Eat soon, while everything is still crunchy and fresh.

Radish Toasts with Pistachio and Green Olive Butter

Do try this toasted pistachio and olive butter with the radishes; it's a slightly more complex version of the simplest radishes with salted butter, but it works exceptionally well.

SERVES 4–6 _____ AS A SUBSTANTIAL CANAPÉ
PREPARATION TIME _____ 20 MINUTES
COOKING TIME _____ 8 MINUTES

50g (1¾oz) unsalted shelled pistachios
50g (1¾oz) very green olives, stoned and chopped
    quite finely
1 tsp finely chopped fresh mint, plus extra leaves
    to serve
75g (2½oz) unsalted butter, very soft
1 small, wholemeal baguette, sliced and toasted
150g (5oz) radishes, sliced paper-thin
salt and freshly ground black pepper

Preheat the oven to 190°C (375°F/gas 5).

Toast the pistachios in a roasting pan for 7–8 minutes until golden and fragrant. Let cool, then chop finely. Combine with the olives, mint and the very soft butter in a bowl, seasoning generously with black pepper and a little salt.

Spread the still-warm, toasted baguette slices with the butter – be extremely generous – and cover with discs of paper-thin radish. Sprinkle with sea salt and more black pepper to serve. That's it.

Vietnamese-Style Omelette Breakfast Salad

Based on the idea of Vietnamese *banh xeo*, a folded, rice flour crêpe, but here in easy, breakfast omelette guise. I'm very keen on the idea of savoury, vegetable or salad-based recipes to start the day, whatever Western convention currently says. It seems so obvious to make breakfast an opportunity for delicious, sustaining food whenever time allows. Admittedly, this would be one for a weekend breakfast for most, practically speaking, but it would also make an excellent light lunch or supper.

SERVES 2

PREPARATION TIME _____ 20 MINUTES
COOKING TIME _____ 10 MINUTES

FOR THE OMELETTES

6 eggs
2 tsp light soy sauce
½ tsp ground turmeric
2 red chillies, finely sliced
5 spring onions (scallions), finely sliced
2 tbsp groundnut (peanut) oil
salt and freshly ground black pepper

FOR THE FILLING

100g (3½oz) beansprouts
4 spring onions (scallions), finely shredded
2 carrots, peeled and shredded into ribbons
1 large handful of Thai basil, coriander (cilantro)
    and mint leaves, in any combination

TO SERVE

1 Romaine lettuce, leaves separated
½ cucumber, sliced
50g (1¾oz) peanuts, toasted and crushed
chilli sauce

Lightly beat the eggs with the soy sauce, turmeric, half of the chilli, half of the spring onions and a little salt and pepper.

Have the filling ingredients ready and to hand before you start to cook the eggs.

For each omelette, put 1 tablespoon of oil in a large, non-stick frying pan (skillet) and warm through over a medium heat. Add a pinch of salt. Ladle half of the egg mixture in, swirling gently around the pan to distribute it evenly. Cook until golden underneath and just set on top. Flip, then transfer to a plate and fill with half of the salad, folding over to enclose in a half-moon. Repeat with the remaining egg mixture to make a second omelette.

Serve with the peanuts, remaining sliced chilli and spring onion and the chilli sauce. Use the lettuce leaves to wrap or contain slices of omelette and salad as you eat, dipping into the chilli sauce and the peanuts.

Spring

Miso Carrot Salad Plate with Crisp Chickpeas and Carrot Hummus

Anyone who likes hummus (isn't that most people?) would be pretty delighted to be presented with this nourishing salad plate for lunch or supper. The hummus cleverly incorporates some of the roasted carrots used elsewhere and the roasted, spiced chickpeas add extra crunch as well as flavour. It reminds me of London's Cranks Café in its heyday. Any variation of crisp, soy- or chilli-roasted seeds would be good in place of the sunflower seeds suggested here, but I love to use sunflower with carrot as they originate from the same family.

VEGAN
SERVES 4
PREPARATION TIME .... 25 MINUTES
COOKING TIME .... 40 MINUTES

1 tbsp white miso paste
juice of 1 large orange
juice and finely grated zest of 2 lemons
1 tbsp honey
1 tsp dried chilli flakes
2 tbsp light soy sauce
2 tbsp toasted sesame oil
12 large carrots (about 1.4kg/3lb), halved
    lengthways, according to size
2 tbsp groundnut (peanut) or sunflower oil
4 tbsp sunflower seeds
1 tsp hot smoked paprika
2 x 400g (14oz) tins of chickpeas (garbanzos),
    rinsed and drained separately, reserving the
    liquid of one tin
2 tbsp well-stirred tahini
2 garlic cloves, roughly chopped
salt and freshly ground black pepper

TO SERVE

1 handful of sunflower sprouts
red chicory (endive) leaves and watercress sprigs
a cooked grain, such as spelt or barley (optional)

Preheat the oven to 200°C (400°F/gas 6).

Make the miso dressing by combining the miso, orange juice, juice of 1 lemon and zest of 2, honey, chilli, soy sauce and sesame oil. Toss 2 tablespoons of this with the carrots and an extra tablespoon of groundnut oil. Roast for 30 minutes.

Scatter the sunflower seeds and paprika over all but 4 carrot halves and roast for a further 10 minutes until the seeds are golden and the carrots tender and caramelized.

Meanwhile, spread one tin of drained chickpeas out on a separate tray with 2 tablespoons of the dressing and 1 tablespoon of groundnut oil. Roast for 20–25 minutes until golden and turning crisp at the edges.

Put the 4 uncoated roasted carrots in a blender with the other tin of chickpeas, plus 4 tablespoons of the liquid saved from the tin, the tahini, garlic and juice of the remaining lemon. Season with salt and pepper and blend until completely smooth and silky.

Serve the roasted carrots with the hummus and sunflower sprouts, accompanied by a salad of chicory and watercress leaves with the cooked grains alongside, if using. Spoon a little of the remaining dressing over each plate.

Spring

NOTE

Sunflower sprouts are available to buy in many supermarkets. If you can't find them, you can substitute with mustard cress or any sprouts/microgreens.

Broad Bean, Butternut, Avocado and Pickled Radish Tostadas

Aren't these tostadas pretty? A celebration of broad (fava) beans, double-podded to show off their spring greens. They taste as good as they are handsome; the pickled radishes and avocado cream being essential components, I feel.

SERVES 4   MAKES 20
PREPARATION TIME   40 MINUTES
COOKING TIME   50 MINUTES

200g (7oz) podded broad (fava) beans
600g (1lb 5oz) butternut squash, cut into
    2cm (¾in) cubes
2 tbsp olive oil
1 tsp dried oregano
2 tsp coriander seeds, crushed
½ tsp dried chilli (hot pepper) flakes
    or smoked paprika
100g (3½oz) radishes, finely sliced
2 tbsp red wine vinegar
½ tsp caster (superfine) sugar
2 large, ripe avocadoes, halved and stoned
juice of 1 large lime
1 handful of coriander (cilantro) leaves
20 x 10cm (4in) diameter fresh corn tortillas
4 spring onions (scallions), trimmed and
    finely shredded
100g (3½oz) Wensleydale or feta cheese, crumbled
salt and freshly ground black pepper

TO SERVE

hot sauce

Blanch the podded broad (fava) beans in boiling water for 1–2 minutes. Drain in a colander, refresh under cool water, then 'double-pod' by nicking the pale green outer skins with a knife and slipping each bright, jewel-green bean out. Chill until needed.

Preheat the oven to 200°C (400°F/gas 6).

Coat the squash in the olive oil, oregano, coriander seeds and chilli or paprika. Roast for 35–40 minutes, until caramelized and tender. Set aside to cool, then combine with the double-podded broad beans.

To pickle the radishes, put them in a non-reactive (china or plastic is ideal) container with the red wine vinegar, sugar and a good pinch of salt. Set aside for 15 minutes.

Put the avocado flesh in a blender with the lime juice and half of the coriander leaves. Blitz to a buttery purée and season to taste, adding extra lime juice if it needs it.

Toast the tortillas in a dry frying pan set over a very high heat, turning with tongs until both sides are toasted and even look slightly charred (in spots). This will take about 1 minute on each side.

Lay the toasted tortillas out on a serving platter or board and top each with a heaped teaspoon of avocado cream, followed by a spoonful of roast squash and broad beans, drained radishes, remaining coriander leaves, spring onions and crumbled cheese. Serve with hot sauce, if liked.

Tofu, Miso and Bean Balls

Is there a more delicate descriptor for these tofu, ginger, seaweed, broad (fava) bean and rice concoctions? 'Falafel' or 'patties' doesn't seem right. Whatever the name, they are unusual, high in protein and delicious, especially when served in salad bowls with pickled cucumber and pickled ginger, avocado, sesame and the like. Sub in 250g (9oz) ready-podded peas for the broad beans if they are more readily available to you or you can't bear the podding process.

A note on broad beans: you'll need about 500–550g (1lb 2–3½oz) in their pods to glean 400g (14oz) shelled-weight beans. This will yield around 250g (9oz) double-podded broad beans. Useful to know as a general guide.

SERVES 4   **MAKES 20–24 BALLS**
PREPARATION TIME   **30 MINUTES**
COOKING TIME   **25 MINUTES**

FOR THE BALLS

400g (14oz) podded broad (fava) beans
450g (1lb) extra-firm tofu, drained and cubed
2 garlic cloves, crushed
20g (¾oz) fresh ginger root, peeled and chopped
2 tbsp white miso paste
250g (9oz) cooked and well-drained wholegrain rice (can be from microwave pack)
2 tbsp nori seaweed flakes
5 spring onions (scallions), trimmed and finely chopped (may need extra shredded to serve)
2 tbsp toasted sesame oil
salt and freshly ground black pepper

FOR THE BOWLS

½ large cucumber, peeled, halved, deseeded and finely diced
30g (1oz) pickled ginger, drained, reserving the pickling liquid
2 tsp wasabi paste
1 tbsp lime juice
4 tbsp mayonnaise
2 large, ripe avocadoes, halved and stoned
50g (1¾oz) watercress sprigs
2 tbsp toasted sesame seeds
6 spring onions (scallions), trimmed and finely shredded

Preheat the oven to 190°C (375°F/gas 5).

Start by tossing the diced cucumber with the pickling liquid drained from the pickled ginger. Set aside.

Blanch the podded broad beans in boiling water for 1–2 minutes. Drain in a colander, refresh under cool water, then 'double-pod' by nicking the pale green outer skins with a knife and slipping each bright, jewel-green bean out. Chill until needed.

To make the tofu balls, put the cubed tofu in the small bowl of a food processor. Blitz until the mixture is smooth and beginning to clump together (1–2 minutes). Now add the garlic, ginger, miso and a generous amount of black pepper with a smaller amount of salt. Blitz again to combine the ingredients and break the ginger down. Finally, add the broad beans, rice, nori flakes and spring onions, blitzing again to chop the broad beans finely enough that the mixture turns a rubbly, pale green. Firmly form into 20–24, large-walnut-sized balls using clean hands.

Place the balls in a large baking pan lined with non-stick baking parchment and drizzle with the oil, turning to coat. Space the balls out evenly. Bake for 25 minutes, until pale golden and sizzling.

Drain any excess liquid from the cucumber, which should now have been sitting for around 30 minutes. Combine the wasabi paste, lime juice and mayonnaise in a bowl.

Serve the balls, hot or cool, in wide bowls accompanied with the avocado halves, watercress, the 'pickled' cucumber, pickled sushi ginger and wasabi mayonnaise. Scatter with sesame seeds and tuck in the shredded spring onions, to finish.

Spring

SUMMER

WHAT'S IN SEASON?

Artichokes

Aubergines (eggplants)

Beetroot (beets)

Broad (fava) beans

Chillies

Courgettes (zucchini)

Early carrots

Fennel

French beans

Garlic

Kohlrabi

Lettuce and salads

Mangetout (snow peas)

New potatoes

Onions

Pak choy (bok choi)

Peas

(Bell) peppers

Pulses (fresh)

Runner beans

Soft herbs

Sorrel

Sweetcorn

Tomatoes

Summer

This is it: the peak of growth and sun-warmed flavours; a bounty of leafy and ripe produce. Summer's harvests of beans and pods mob the vines from which they spring. Beets are small and sugared, as are baby carrots in natty colourways; garlic is purple, plump and mild, to be crushed into everything; tomatoes taste of themselves again. Much of the crop is plentiful in volume, but diminutive in form. That is to say that bulging handfuls of peas and broad (fava) beans are more typical than the bold, centrepiece offerings of colder months, such as cauliflowers or butternuts. This makes for 'busier' plates: more salads that are jumbled and muddled together, more griddle lines and barbecue flashes tumbled onto platters than long oven stints and baking dishes. There will be plenty of time for that later.

Slow-Roast Fennel with Lemon and Fennel Seed Gremolata

A wintery cooking method made summer-friendly with a vibrant gremolata. The fennel will turn to a sweet confit in its fragrant oil bath, making a beautiful vegetable side, bruschetta topping, pasta sauce (when roughly chopped) or even a main event, accompanied by a peppery leaf salad and a wedge of frittata or good cheese. Swap the honey for maple syrup or agave to make this vegan.

SERVES 4 .... **AS A SIDE**
PREPARATION TIME .... **15 MINUTES**
COOKING TIME .... **1 HOUR 30 MINUTES**

2 tsp fennel seeds
3 fennel bulbs, trimmed and cut into sixths, reserving any fronds
3 tbsp extra virgin olive oil
5 lemon thyme or thyme sprigs
2 tsp honey
juice of 1 small lemon
finely grated zest of 2 small lemons
2 garlic cloves, very finely chopped
1 small bunch of flat-leaf parsley, finely chopped
1 red chilli, finely chopped
salt and freshly ground black pepper

Preheat the oven to 170°C (340°F/gas 3).

Put the fennel seeds in a small frying pan (skillet) set over a medium heat and toast for a minute or so until a shade darker and fragrant but not overly toasted. Crush roughly and set aside.

Put the fennel wedges in a large baking dish or roasting pan with the oil, thyme sprigs, honey and lemon juice. Season with salt and pepper, cover with kitchen foil and roast for 1 hour 10 minutes. Remove the foil and turn the fennel wedges over. Return to the oven for a further 20 minutes.

Meanwhile, combine the chopped garlic with the parsley, chilli, fennel seeds and any reserved fennel fronds. Season with salt and pepper and scatter this mixture over the hot or cooled caramelized fennel to serve.

Summer Beans with Green Chilli Dressing and Pistachios

This salad makes an excellent barbecue side or mezze component. All the summer beans – green and yellow variations of round beans for preference, but runner will work too – are generously cloaked with a hot, verdant dressing, made ahead of time and loosely based on the Yemeni *zhug* or *zhoug*. The pistachios are not an authentic addition, nor is the dash of honey, included to balance the fire. Possibly not one for kids as the raw, green chillies bring a stealthy heat.

SERVES 4	AS A SIDE
PREPARATION TIME	25 MINUTES
COOKING TIME	5 MINUTES

FOR THE DRESSING

1 tsp cumin seeds, toasted and crushed
8 large green chillies, stalks removed and
    roughly sliced
3 fat garlic cloves, roughly chopped
1 small bunch of flat-leaf parsley, including stalks,
    plus extra leaves to serve
1 small bunch of coriander (cilantro),
    including stalks
3 green cardamom pods, bruised and seeds removed
3 tbsp lemon juice
2 tsp mild honey
4 tbsp extra virgin olive oil, plus extra to serve
salt and freshly ground black pepper

FOR THE SALAD

700g (1lb 9oz) mixed summer beans (see intro),
    trimmed
500g (1lb 2oz) jar of labneh balls in olive oil,
    drained
50g (1¾oz) nibbed or chopped pistachios,
    lightly toasted

To make the *zhoug*-style dressing, blitz all the ingredients together in a blender or food processor with 3 tablespoons of water and salt and pepper to taste. Cover and chill for up to 24 hours until needed, bringing up to room temperature to use.

Blanch the beans in plenty of boiling, salted water for 4–5 minutes, or until just tender. This will depend on their size and thickness, so keep an eye and batch them up if wildly different in size or variety. Refresh under cool water in a colander, drain well and tip onto a platter with the drained rounds of labneh. Dress liberally and drizzle with more extra virgin olive oil to taste, scattering with the pistachios and perhaps some extra parsley leaves to serve.

Summer

Summer

Roasted Carrot and Chickpea Patties with Basil-Feta Pesto

The 'pesto' (stretching the term a bit here) can also be spread on garlicky, toasted bread and topped with roasted – or the sweetest fresh – tomatoes. Or toss it through warm, roasted root vegetables as a punchy dressing.

SERVES 4	WITH ACCOMPANIMENTS
MAKES	16–20 PATTIES
PREPARATION TIME	25 MINUTES
COOKING TIME	40 MINUTES

FOR THE FETA AND BASIL PESTO

1 large garlic clove, chopped
2 small bunches of basil
5 tbsp extra virgin olive oil
finely grated zest and 3 tbsp juice of 1 lemon
100g (3½oz) feta, crumbled
salt and freshly ground black pepper

FOR THE PATTIES

750g (1lb 10oz) medium carrots, scrubbed
4½ tbsp olive oil
1 red onion, finely sliced
2 garlic cloves, crushed
½ tsp dried chilli (hot pepper) flakes
1½ tsp cumin seeds
2 x 400g (14oz) tins of chickpeas (garbanzos), well drained
1 small bunch of flat-leaf parsley, with stalks, finely chopped
1 small bunch of basil leaves
finely grated zest of 1 lemon
2 tbsp chickpea or gram flour
100g (3½oz) feta, crumbled

TO SERVE

salad leaves
4 lemon wedges
warm paper-thin flatbreads

To make the basil-feta pesto, pulse all the ingredients except the feta together in a mini food processor. Add the feta and pulse again to break it down a little. Season to taste, being mindful of salt levels.

Preheat the oven to 200°C (400°F/gas 6).

Coat the carrots with 1½ tablespoons of the oil and spread out in a roasting pan. Roast for about 40 minutes until soft and beginning to turn golden all over, then roughly crush half of them.

Reduce the oven temperature to 190°C (375°F/gas 5).

Soften the sliced onion in a frying pan (skillet) in 1 tablespoon of the oil for 10 minutes over a medium heat, adding the garlic, chilli flakes and cumin seeds for the final minute. Tip into a food processor with the drained chickpeas, parsley and stalks, a small handful of basil leaves, the lemon zest, chickpea flour, the crushed roasted carrots and lots of black pepper. Pulse to a rough paste, stopping to scrape down the sides, then add 50g (1¾oz) of the crumbled feta and pulse again to just combine. If possible, chill the mixture for at least 30 minutes or up to 24 hours before forming into 16–20 patties; this will firm it up and make the patties much easier to pan-fry neatly.

Using a large frying pan set over medium heat, fry the patties in two batches, using 1 tablespoon of olive oil per batch and cooking for 3–4 minutes on each side until golden. Alternatively, brush the patties with a total of 2 tablespoons of olive oil, space out on a lined baking (cookie) sheet and bake in the oven for 20–25 minutes.

Serve with the feta and basil pesto, the remaining whole roasted carrots, salad leaves, lemon wedges and warmed flatbreads.

Summer Lasagne

Not one for purists, I'm afraid – it has no sauce, for a start – but this summer-supper-friendly version is stacked with character from the roast Mediterranean-style vegetables and their spiced coating of dukkah, paprika and coriander seeds. By all means cheat and use a bought, fresh pesto, but if you do want to make your own, there's a template recipe on page 218. I'd go for the kale and hazelnut variation here; the flavours suit it.

SERVES 4–6 .... WITH SALAD
PREPARATION TIME .... 30 MINUTES
COOKING TIME .... 1 HOUR 25 MINUTES

4 large courgettes (zucchini), trimmed and sliced
6 large, sweet (bell) peppers, cored and sliced into thick 'cheeks'
2 aubergines (eggplants), halved lengthways and sliced into 1cm (½in) thick half-moons
4 tbsp extra virgin olive oil, plus extra for the dish
4 heaped tsp dukkah
1 tsp hot paprika
2 tsp coriander seeds, roughly crushed
150g fresh pesto, preferably the kale and hazelnut on page 218 in Sauces
500g (1lb 2oz) ricotta cheese, drained
375g (13oz) fresh lasagne sheets
1 small bunch of basil, leaves torn
2 x 125g (4oz) balls of buffalo mozzarella, drained and roughly torn
90g (3oz) vegetarian pecorino or hard cheese, finely grated
salt and freshly ground black pepper

TO SERVE
peppery green salad

Preheat the oven to 200°C (400°F/gas 6).

Put the vegetables in a large bowl and toss with the oil, dukkah, paprika and coriander seeds, seasoning generously with salt and pepper as you do so. Divide between 2–3 large roasting pans, making sure the vegetables are spaced out well and in single layers. Roast for about 40 minutes until soft and beginning to colour. Set aside. This step can be completed up to 48 hours ahead of time; keep the vegetables covered and chilled, bringing them up to room temperature before assembling the lasagne.

To put the lasagne together, lightly oil a 20 x 30cm (8 x 12in) ovenproof dish. Start with a spoonful of pesto, spreading it out over the base and dotting with heaped teaspoons of ricotta, seasoning as you go. Cover with a single layer of lasagne sheets, followed by a layer of roast vegetables and torn basil leaves, covering these with more pasta sheets.

Continue in this order until all the ingredients are used up, finishing with a layer of pasta covered with the final topping of torn mozzarella and grated pecorino. Bake for about 40–45 minutes until golden and bubbling. Serve with a peppery green salad.

Summer Vegetable Pakoras

I rarely recommend deep-frying at home, so trust these gluten-free, spiced pakoras are worth the hype and relative faff. They can be made with almost any delicate or thinly sliced seasonal vegetables, such as late asparagus, green beans, onions, early mushrooms, new potatoes, carrot, beetroot (beets) ...

VEGAN

SERVES 4	AS A SNACK OR STARTER
PREPARATION TIME	30 MINUTES
RESTING	AT LEAST 2 HOURS
COOKING TIME	10 MINUTES

FOR THE CHICKPEA PAKORA BATTER

75ml (2½fl oz) vegetable oil
4 fat garlic cloves, finely chopped
1¼ tsp sea salt
2 tsp garam masala
1½ tsp ground turmeric
1 tsp chilli powder
2 tsp cumin seeds, toasted
2 tsp baking powder
230g (8oz) chickpea (gram) flour
230ml (8fl oz) warm water
1 small bunch of coriander (cilantro), including
    stalks, very finely chopped
salt and freshly ground black pepper

FOR THE PAKORAS

1 bunch of slender spring onions (scallions),
    sliced into 4–5cm (1½–2in) lengths
2 baby courgettes (zucchini), sliced into fine
    matchsticks
1 small sweet potato, sliced into fine matchsticks
100g (3½oz) tenderstem or standard broccoli,
    torn into small florets
50g (1¾oz) podded peas
100g (3½oz) sugarsnap peas or mangetout
    (snow peas), halved lengthways
1 litre (34fl oz) vegetable oil, to deep-fry

TO SERVE

4 heaped tbsp mango chutney or chilli jam
extra coriander leaves (optional)
lime wedges (optional)

To make the batter, combine all the ingredients except the coriander in a blender or food processor and blitz to a smooth mixture, seasoning with plenty of black pepper. (You can blitz in the coriander for no more than 2 seconds at this point, just to finely chop the herbs, not to turn the batter a sludgy green – chopping it and stirring it in with the vegetables avoids the risk.) Cover the batter and set aside to settle for a couple of hours or chill overnight. It will keep well for 48 hours or so.

When you are ready to cook, preheat the oven to its lowest setting, ready to keep the first cooked pakoras warm. Stir the batter well. Combine the prepared vegetables with the batter in a large bowl. It shouldn't need any extra salt as the batter is heavily seasoned and you can always scatter with a little more after cooking.

Put the oil in a large, deep-sided saucepan and set over a low-medium heat to heat up slowly. The oil should be at 180°C (350°F) on a thermometer or take about 25 seconds to turn a cube of white bread golden-brown.

Carefully drop heaped tablespoons of the mixture into the hot oil to make 5–6 pakoras in a batch, spacing them out well. Fry for 3–4 minutes, turning with a slotted spoon until golden all over. Remove to a plate lined with paper towel to drain off any excess oil. Transfer to the low oven while you repeat the process with the rest of the batter.

Accompany the hot pakoras with mango chutney to dip, and coriander sprigs and lime wedges for squeezing over, if you like. Eat them as soon as possible after cooking, while they are still crisp and delicious.

Pak Choy, Miso and Mushroom Noodle Bowls

Be aware of using overly salty stock in the soup base here, throwing off the balance between the aromatics and the miso paste; if in doubt, simply use water and adjust the miso to add more depth. Sheets of dried kombu seaweed are available in health food shops – add one with the stock and remove before serving to add an extra layer of umami. I haven't included one here as I try to keep the specialist ingredients to a minimum.

You might want more protein, in which case I'd suggest an egg – softly boiled and gently peeled, or softly poached – added to the bowl just before eating. A few slices of salty, fried tofu are also welcome.

SERVES 4
PREPARATION TIME .... 20 MINUTES
COOKING TIME .... 35 MINUTES

2 medium leeks, trimmed and sliced
1 tbsp groundnut (peanut) oil
2 large garlic cloves, sliced
2 tbsp finely chopped fresh ginger root
15g (½oz) dried shiitake mushrooms, crumbled or broken up roughly
1 litre (34fl oz) light vegetable stock
2 tbsp mirin, to taste
1 tbsp white miso paste
4 small heads pak choy (bok choi), trimmed and leaves separated
200g (7oz) oyster mushrooms, roughly shredded
200g (7oz) ramen noodles, cooked and drained

TO SERVE

2 sheets of toasted nori seaweed, snipped into pieces or strips
2 tbsp pickled daikon or shredded fresh radish
4 spring onions (scallions), finely shredded
2 tbsp sriracha sauce
tofu (optional)
soft-boiled or poached egg, halved (optional)

Soften the sliced leeks in the oil in a large saucepan (skillet) or ovenproof casserole set over a low heat. It should take about 10 minutes of gentle cooking, stirring often, for the leeks to become very soft and sweet. Add the garlic and ginger, cooking for a further 2 minutes. Now add the crumbled shiitake, the stock and mirin to the pan with 300ml (10fl oz) of water. Bring up to the boil, then reduce the heat and simmer gently, uncovered, for 20 minutes.

Stir in the miso and taste. Is the stock concentrated enough? Is it too strong? This is the time to reduce it or add more water, as needed. If you feel the soup base needs more sweetness, add an extra slosh of mirin. Once you're happy with the flavours, add the green vegetables and fresh mushrooms and simmer for 5 minutes, or until the mushrooms are soft.

Meanwhile, cook the noodles in boiling water according to the packet instructions, then drain.

Divide the cooked noodles between warmed serving bowls and ladle the soup over the top. Add any extras you like to pep up the bowls: snipped nori seaweed, shredded radish or pickled daikon, shredded spring onions and/or a dollop of chilli sauce. This would also be the ideal time to tuck in a soft-boiled egg or a few slices of golden tofu, as suggested in the introduction.

Charred Runner Beans
on a Walnut Tarator

This is a superb summer barbecue recipe. The whole beans are charred straight on a barbecue or smoking-hot griddle/frying pan; no pre-steaming needed, just brush with oil and whack them on. Runner, Helda or any similarly shaped and sized whole beans will work; they respond beautifully, blistering and softening in minutes. Pile the beans over a garlicky 'tarator' sauce of creamy walnuts and lemon for an easy side with the big impact of Eastern European and Middle Eastern flavours.

VEGAN

SERVES 4	AS A SIDE
PREPARATION TIME	20 MINUTES
COOKING TIME	15 MINUTES

150g (5oz) walnut halves, 50g (1½oz) reserved after toasting, 100g (3½oz) in tarator
1 garlic clove, roughly chopped
finely pared zest and juice of 1 lemon
50g (1¾oz) sliced crustless white sourdough, soaked in water for 5 minutes
3 tbsp extra virgin olive oil, plus extra to serve
about 700g (1lb 9oz) runner beans or other bean varieties of similar shape and size, stalks trimmed and any tough side strings removed
1 handful of fennel fronds or fresh dill, chopped
salt and freshly ground black pepper

TO SERVE
2 lemon wedges (optional)

The tarator can be made up to 4 days ahead of time and chilled. Just let it down with a little warm water to serve as it will thicken up as it sits.

To make it, toast the walnuts in a dry frying pan (skillet) set over a medium heat for about 4 minutes, tossing the pan to keep the nuts moving. They should be golden and fragrant. Set aside to cool slightly.

Put the garlic in a mini food processor with 100g (3½oz) of the walnuts, the lemon juice, the sourdough, 1 tablespoon of the olive oil and 75ml (2½fl oz) water. Blitz to a thick, creamy sauce, adding a little more water if needed, to get the blades moving. Season with salt and pepper.

Either have a griddle pan ready or a barbecue with white-hot coals and a metal grid in place. Toss the whole beans and courgette ribbons with the remaining 2 tablespoons of olive oil and season well. Griddle in a smoking-hot pan set over a high heat, or over the coals, turning with tongs every couple of minutes, until the vegetables are slightly charred all over. This will take about 4 minutes on each side.

Spread the walnut sauce on a platter and arrange the beans on top, drizzling with extra virgin olive oil and scattering with herbs and lemon zest. Squeeze the lemon wedges over to finish, if liked.

Summer

Globe Artichokes with Tomato, Saffron and Garlic

Generous quantities of butter are warranted, necessary even, when dipping globe artichoke leaves and hearts; though of course you can substitute good olive oil. The saffron, tomato and toasted almonds make this starter or indulgent lunch luxurious in flavour, but I don't recommend the home cook gets overly concerned with complicated artichoke prep. The instructions here are as simple as can be, recommending minimal trimming and removal of the central choke after cooking. The 'petals' can then be pulled away, dipping their bulbous bases in butter before eating until the tender heart is revealed – eat this with a knife and fork. Serve with sourdough and perhaps a simply dressed salad of peppery leaves and goat's cheese if you want more on the table.

SERVES 4

PREPARATION TIME	30 MINUTES
COOKING TIME	35 MINUTES

4 large globe artichokes, trimmed
1 lemon, halved
1 large pinch of saffron strands
100g (3½oz) salted butter
2 large garlic cloves, finely sliced
2 red chillies, finely sliced
50g (1¾oz/2 tbsp) flaked (slivered) almonds, toasted
400g (14oz) flavourful, ripe tomatoes, diced
1½ tbsp sherry vinegar
2 tbsp finely chopped chives
salt and freshly ground black pepper

TO SERVE

good-quality bread

Use a sharp, serrated knife to cut a slice about 2cm (¾in) thick from the top of each artichoke flower (actually a thistle). Trim the stalks to about 5cm (2in) long, paring the outer layer of stalk away and removing any stray, low leaves. Drop the artichokes into a bowl of cool water with the lemon halves squeezed into the water (add these too). This will prevent the artichokes oxidizing and turning black.

Choose a saucepan large enough to hold all the artichokes in one layer. Fill it with water and bring it to a boil, then add the artichokes. Simmer for 30–35 minutes, or until tender (very large artichokes can take up to 45 minutes). Remove the central, hairy chokes with a teaspoon, pulling back the central leaves to reach them. I find it easier to do this after cooking as the raw artichokes are so tough, but you can take it out at the initial prep stage if you prefer.

While the artichokes are simmering, make the butter. Put the saffron in a cup and add 2 tablespoons of just-boiled water. Set aside to steep for 10 minutes.

Melt the butter in a small saucepan set over a low heat. Add the garlic, chillies and almonds and cook very gently for 8–10 minutes, by which time the garlic should have softened in flavour but not coloured. Now add the tomatoes, sherry vinegar, the saffron in its water and the chives. Continue to heat through very gently for 5 minutes. Season generously with black pepper and sparsely with salt.

Serve the warm, choke-less artichokes in shallow bowls, with the tomato butter spooned into their middles. Offer bread alongside, plus finger bowls and empty bowls for the artichoke petals.

Tomato, Lemongrass and Peanut Noodles

This is an excellent little supper recipe to have on stand-by. For some reason, tomatoes are a standard combination with quick pastas, but not noodles. I love them here for their sweetness and sauce-y texture, with toasted peanuts, lemongrass and other aromatics, plus a good kick of chilli.

For preference, I'd recommend using Taifun's smoked almond tofu here. It's widely available and has a salty, savoury flavour and extremely firm texture, perfect for flipping around a wok. Otherwise, use any extra-firm smoked tofu.

SERVES 2

PREPARATION TIME	20 MINUTES
COOKING TIME	10 MINUTES

180g (6¼oz/2 sheets) dried wholewheat egg noodles
2 tbsp groundnut (peanut) or other flavourless oil
4 shallots, halved and very finely sliced
3 lemongrass stalks, trimmed and finely sliced
2 red chillies, sliced
1 large thumb of fresh ginger root, peeled and finely sliced
400g (14oz) small cherry tomatoes, mixed varieties if possible
2 large garlic cloves, finely sliced
1 small bunch of coriander (cilantro), chopped, including the stalks
200g (7oz) firm smoked tofu, diced
2 tsp palm sugar or brown sugar
2 tbsp light soy sauce
juice of 1 lime
60g (2oz) peanuts, toasted and roughly crushed

Have all your ingredients prepared and on-hand. You want to keep the heat very high and the wok or frying pan (skillet) moving near constantly once the stir-frying starts.

Simmer the noodles in salted water for 3 minutes, then drain in a colander, refreshing under cold water and gently prising apart. If they're going to be sitting for longer than a few minutes, toss with a dash of oil to prevent them sticking together.

Put the oil in a large wok or deep frying pan (skillet) set over a high heat. Add the shallots and stir-fry briskly for 3–4 minutes. Now throw in the lemongrass, chilli and ginger, moving around the pan for another minute before adding the tomatoes. Keep everything on the move (by tossing and shimmying the pan, restaurant style, if that's a talent you possess). Throw in the garlic, coriander stalks, tofu and sugar. Keep everything stir-frying and moving for a few minutes until the tomatoes begin to collapse (the back of a spoon to crush slightly will help out here) and the sugar begins to caramelize. The shallots should be properly frazzled and highly coloured by this point.

Add the soy sauce and lime juice and bubble down for a few seconds before tossing through the noodles, most of the coriander leaves and half of the peanuts. Divide between bowls and top with the remaining coriander leaves and peanuts.

Summer

Cucumber, Watermelon, Baked Feta and Olive Salad

A twist on what has become a summer classic: watermelon, olive and feta, with cucumber taking on a pivotal role as our salad veg here. Swap in diced halloumi as the baked cheese and add mint instead of basil. You can also bake a handful of torn sourdough alongside the cheese, tossing it in a little extra oil first.

No cooked watermelon here because I'm yet to be convinced that griddling or grilling the fruit does anything but coax out a vile, chemical taste. Fresh, raw and juicy is the only way to serve it as far as I'm concerned.

SERVES 4
PREPARATION TIME .... **25 MINUTES**
COOKING TIME .... **15 MINUTES**

200g (7oz) feta, drained and cut into
   3cm (1¼in) cubes
5 tbsp extra virgin olive oil
1 small red onion, very finely sliced into rounds
50g (1¾oz) stoned Greek black olives
1 tsp dried oregano (or use 5 sprigs, leaves stripped)
½ tsp dried chilli (hot pepper) flakes
1 tsp mild honey
2–3 tbsp red wine vinegar
700g (1lb 9oz) watermelon flesh (no rind), sliced
   into chunks
1 medium cucumber, peeled, deseeded and sliced
1 small pomegranate, arils only
1 tsp sumac (optional)
1 small handful of basil, leaves shredded if large
salt and freshly ground black pepper

Preheat the oven to 200°C (400°F/gas 6).

Gently toss the feta in a roasting pan with 2 tablespoons of the olive oil, the onion, olives, dried oregano and chilli. Season with pepper but no salt yet. Roast for 12–15 minutes until the onion is *just* soft and frazzled at the edges.

Combine the remaining 3 tablespoons of oil with the honey and 2 tablespoons of red wine vinegar (you can add a further tablespoon once the salad is assembled, if needed. It depends on how sweet the watermelon is).

Combine the watermelon, cucumber, pomegranate arils and all but a few basil leaves on a serving platter. Scatter the feta mixture over and gently toss through, being careful not to break up the feta. Add the oil and vinegar mixture to the empty feta pan to catch any dressing there. Taste and add the extra vinegar if your watermelon is particularly sweet, adding a little salt too, if needed... again remembering the feta is salty. Balance is key. Spoon this dressing over the salad and shower with the sumac, if using, followed by the remaining basil leaves.

Baked Courgette and Pea Spirals
with Halloumi and Tomato

This recipe was inspired by an uncredited picture of baked, courgette pinwheels on Pinterest. I've little clue what the original roll-ups contained – these are a muddle of peas, spinach and ricotta with summer herbs and salty halloumi, baked in a cinnamon-spiced tomato sauce – but I loved the idea, even if it is a little fiddly to construct. To compensate for the careful rolling of courgette ribbons, the dish can be made a few hours or a day ahead of time and kept chilled, ready to bake, or even cooked through and served at room temperature on a hot day.

SERVES 4
PREPARATION TIME _____ 30 MINUTES
COOKING TIME _____ 1 HOUR 25 MINUTES

700g (1lb 9oz) tomato passata (sieved tomatoes)
4 tbsp extra virgin olive oil
3 garlic cloves, crushed
1 cinnamon stick, halved
4 large, fat courgettes (zucchini), trimmed
4 spring onions (scallions), trimmed and sliced
375g (13oz) shelled fresh peas, or you can
    use frozen
120g (4oz) baby spinach leaves
250g (9oz) ricotta, well-drained
250g (9oz) halloumi, drained and coarsely grated
4 heaped tbsp green olive tapenade
1 small handful of basil leaves, chopped
1 small handful of mint leaves, chopped
salt and freshly ground black pepper

TO SERVE
green salad and bread (optional)

Preheat the oven to 190°C (375°F/gas 5).

To make the tomato sauce, put the passata, 2 tablespoons of the oil, 2 crushed garlic cloves and the cinnamon sticks in a 23cm (9in) diameter round or 25cm (10in) square ovenproof dish. Bake in the middle of the oven for about 25 minutes until browning at the edges and reduced in volume slightly. Set aside.

Using a wide vegetable peeler or a mandoline, pare the courgettes into wide ribbons from top to bottom (about 2mm/^{1}/sin thick). There should be 35–40 full-width ribbons in total. Work on getting 8–10 per courgette. Toss with 1 tablespoon of oil. Chop the remaining, unused pieces of courgette as finely as possible – tiny dice are ideal here.

Soften the sliced spring onions and finely chopped courgette leftovers in the remaining tablespoon of oil in a large saucepan set over a lowish heat, stirring often; this should take about 5 minutes. Add the remaining crushed garlic clove and cook for a minute more, followed by the peas with a tablespoon or so of water. Cover with a lid and cook gently for 4–5 minutes to cook the peas, then add the spinach and stir through for a minute or so until the spinach wilts and any liquid evaporates. Tip the pea mixture into a large bowl and let cool for at least 10 minutes.

Gently stir the ricotta, halloumi and chopped basil and mint into the pea mixture. Season with black pepper and minimal salt.

Remove the cinnamon sticks from the sauce dish and season the sauce with salt and pepper to taste, remembering there will be considerable salt added later by the tapenade and halloumi.

Lay the courgette ribbons out on a chopping board in a single layer (you'll be repeating this step until all the courgette has been used). Spread a dab of tapenade over

each ribbon, then add about a tablespoon of the pea mixture to one end of each, spreading it about halfway down the length of the slice as best you can. Now roll up from the filling end, sitting each one, spiral-side up, in the tomato sauce. Repeat to use all the courgettes, tapenade and filling, arranging the spirals in one snug layer in the dish. There should be 35–40 in total, but due to the variety of courgette sizes around, this won't be an exact science!

Bake for about 45 minutes until the sauce is bubbling and the courgettes are tender and turning golden on top. Let cool for 10 minutes before scattering with the reserved basil and mint leaves. Serve hot, warm or at room temperature. Accompany with a green salad and perhaps some warm bread, lentils or rice.

Baked Romano Peppers Stuffed with Giant Vegetable Couscous

An unassuming baked pepper at first glance, but these are big on luscious, sweet vegetable and umami flavours. If you can, make them in advance to give the stuffing a chance to settle, serving as more of a salad or an antipasti, perhaps with blocks of feta, baked with oregano and chilli, plus a green salad or stir-fried greens.

VEGAN
SERVES 4
PREPARATION TIME .... 25 MINUTES
COOKING TIME .... 1 HOUR 30 MINUTES

FOR THE PEPPERS

8 large Romano peppers
1 tbsp olive oil to coat, plus extra for drizzling

FOR THE COUSCOUS

3 tbsp olive oil
1 sweet onion, finely chopped
2 courgettes (zucchini), finely diced
2 tsp coriander seeds, crushed
200g (7oz) wholegrain giant or Israeli couscous
2 tsp thyme leaves, plus a few extra sprigs to serve
1 heaped tbsp tomato purée (paste)
1 tsp sweet smoked paprika
2 garlic cloves, chopped
300ml (10fl oz) vegetable stock
2 tbsp sherry vinegar
salt and freshly ground black pepper

Preheat the oven to 220°C (425°F/gas 7).

Toss the peppers with the oil to coat lightly, then place in a roasting pan in one layer. Roast for 15 minutes, then use tongs to transfer 4 of the peppers to a plate and set aside. Turn the remaining peppers over in the pan and continue to roast for 10–15 minutes until charred in places and soft. Tip into a bowl and cover with a plate, setting aside to steam for 10 minutes or so. Peel these peppers and discard any seeds, core and stalks, then chop the flesh roughly.

Turn the oven down to 180°C (350°F/ gas 4).

Meanwhile prepare the couscous. Put the oil in a medium saucepan set over a lowish heat and add the onion and courgettes with a pinch of salt. Cook, stirring often, for at least 15 minutes. Add the coriander seeds and couscous and really toast for a minute or two, with the heat turned up a notch. Now add the thyme leaves, tomato purée, paprika and garlic, stirring through for a minute, followed by the stock. Cover and simmer the couscous for 12 minutes until just tender.

Add the vinegar and chopped, roasted peppers off the heat. Let cool a little, then use this mixture to stuff the whole peppers, first cutting a long slit on one side and removing any seeds and core (leaving the stalks intact). Make sure the peppers enclose the stuffing as much as possible, but don't worry about being too neat. Nestle them in a roasting pan, drizzle with a little more oil and bake for 20–25 minutes until soft. They will be very delicate so transfer from the dish carefully when the time comes.

Scatter with a few thyme sprigs and serve warm or cool, with salad leaves or as part of a mezze spread. The flavours will settle to your advantage if made up to 48 hours in advance and brought up to room temperature to serve.

Summer

Spinach and Chickpea Dhal
with Charred Courgettes and Okra

A summer or autumn supper, made with plenty of veg and chickpeas (garbanzos) because dhal doesn't have to be lentil-based. Make it ahead of time to let the flavours settle, reheating as needed and brightening with the lemon juice just before serving.

VEGAN
SERVES 4
PREPARATION TIME .... 20 MINUTES
COOKING TIME .... 1 HOUR 10 MINUTES

2 large banana shallots, finely chopped
3 tbsp groundnut (peanut) oil
2 heaped tbsp finely chopped fresh ginger root
3 garlic cloves, finely chopped
2 tsp finely chopped fresh turmeric or
   ½ tsp ground turmeric
2 tsp ground coriander
2 tsp ground cumin
½–1 tsp dried chilli (hot pepper) flakes, to taste
2 tsp garam masala
6 green cardamom pods, lightly crushed
500g (1lb 2oz) cooked chickpeas (garbanzos) or
   2 x 400g (14oz) tins of chickpeas, drained
400g (14oz) flavourful tomatoes, roughly chopped
400ml (13fl oz) tin of coconut milk
4 baby courgettes (zucchini), trimmed and sliced
175g (6oz) okra (ladies' fingers), trimmed and sliced
1 tsp mustard seeds
1 red chilli, sliced
3 tbsp lemon juice
200g (7oz) leaf spinach
salt and freshly ground black pepper

TO SERVE

1 handful of coriander (cilantro) sprigs (optional)
chapati, naan or steamed rice

Sauté the shallots and a pinch of salt in 2 tablespoons of the oil in a large saucepan set over a low-medium heat. After about 8 minutes they should be soft and sweet but not coloured. Add the ginger, garlic and turmeric. Cook, stirring, for 1–2 minutes, then add the remaining spices – being careful with the chilli flakes if you prefer mild heat – and cook for a minute more. Add the chickpeas, chopped tomatoes and coconut milk, refilling the empty tin with water twice and adding it to the pan (a further 800ml/28fl oz of water). Season with salt and pepper.

Bring to the boil, then reduce the heat and simmer for about 50–55 minutes, stirring often to make sure the chickpeas do not catch underneath. They should now be extremely soft so use a potato masher or the back of a spoon to crush about half of them down, thickening the dhal. Alternatively, use a stick blender very sparingly to achieve a similar result, or blitz a couple of ladelfuls of dhal in an upright blender, then return it to the pan. Adjust the consistency as needed, adding a little more water if the dhal seems too thick, or bubbling down briskly for a few minutes if too watery.

Meanwhile, heat the remaining tablespoon of oil in a large frying pan (skillet) set over a very high heat. Add the courgettes and okra, stir-frying aggressively until well-browned and crisp (about 5 minutes); they can stand to be a bit charred in places; don't be afraid of a fierce heat.

Add the mustard seeds and chilli and cook for another 1–2 minutes until the seeds begin to splutter and pop. Season with salt, pepper and a tablespoon of lemon juice off the heat. Set aside.

Stir in the spinach and simmer, stirring often, for 2 minutes until the leaves have wilted down. Finish with the remaining lemon juice to brighten the flavours and spoon the courgette and okra mixture over the top.

Summer

Raw Courgette Salad with Salted Ricotta

Mild Cypriot salted ricotta is excellent with the sweet and fragrant dressing and delicate courgette (zucchini) slices here; but you can substitute with a young pecorino, halloumi or hard goat's cheese. If simmering the lentils from scratch, you'll need about 200g (7oz) raw weight.

SERVES 4
PREPARATION TIME .... **50 MINUTES**

600g (1lb 5oz) courgettes (zucchini), trimmed
finely sliced zest and juice of 1 large lemon
2–3 tsp honey, to taste
5 tbsp extra virgin olive oil
2 red chillies, finely chopped
2 tsp marjoram or oregano leaves, chopped
200g (7oz) salted Cypriot ricotta, thinly sliced
400g (14oz) cooked Puy lentils
1 handful of basil leaves, torn if large
salt and freshly ground black pepper

Shave the courgettes into fine slices using a mandoline or a very sharp knife. Place in a colander with a large pinch of salt, toss through gently and set aside in the sink for 20–40 minutes. Pat dry with a clean tea (dish) towel.

Make the dressing by combining the lemon juice with the honey (to taste), olive oil, chopped chilli and marjoram or oregano. Season to taste (adjust the honey here, if liked).

To make the salad, toss the dried courgettes with the ricotta, lentils and basil leaves on a platter. Drizzle with the dressing and serve.

Summer

Green Bean Thoran

This is a simple version of a *thoran*, inspired by the dry, coconut-based *thorans* of Kerala. The coriander (cilantro) isn't necessarily traditional and can be left out. Think of it as an aromatic, spiced stir-fry, rather than a curry. As well as suiting most barbecues as a side, this makes a low-key supper when accompanied by steamed rice; add a substantial curry and chutneys to make a proper meal.

VEGAN
SERVES 4 AS A SIDE OR WITH RICE AS A MAIN
PREPARATION TIME 10 MINUTES
COOKING TIME 15 MINUTES

90g (3oz) fresh coconut, shaved with a peeler
350g (12oz) mixed green beans and/or runner
    beans, trimmed and cut into smaller pieces
    if large
2 tbsp groundnut (peanut) oil
2 small shallots, finely chopped
20g (¾oz) fresh turmeric, finely chopped
½ tsp mustard seeds (any colour)
1–2 red chillies, finely sliced
12 fresh curry leaves
½ lime
1 handful of coriander (cilantro) leaves,
    roughly chopped
salt and freshly ground black pepper

Spread the coconut out in a large, dry frying pan (skillet) and toast over a medium heat, shaking the pan often until it has lost its 'oily' look and turned an even golden colour. Set aside.

Blanch the beans in plenty of boiling water for 3–4 minutes until just tender. Refresh in a colander under running cool water and drain well.

Put the groundnut oil in the same pan, set over a medium heat again and add the shallots and turmeric. Fry, stirring, for 5 minutes until beginning to soften. Add the mustard seeds, chilli(es) and the beans to the pan and turn the heat up to high, stir-frying and tossing around the pan for 2–3 minutes until the mustard seeds begin to pop. Add the curry leaves for a final minute, season with salt and pepper and remove the pan from the heat. Squeeze the lime juice over the top, then scatter with coconut and coriander. Serve as a side.

Courgette-Sweetcorn Fritters with Pickled Salsa

A fritter for making use of high-summer bounty, homegrown or not, and a good strategy for getting more colourful vegetables on the plate generally – veg fritters go so well with chopped salsas (such as the lightly pickled cucumber one below) and leafy/tomato/lentil/wholegrain/potato salads. Swap in any plain (all-purpose) flour for the chickpea flour, as needed, but chickpea is notable for its flavour, marginally higher protein content and gluten-free credentials.

SERVES 2	MAKES 6–8 FRITTERS
PREPARATION TIME	30 MINUTES
COOKING TIME	10 MINUTES

FOR THE PICKLED SALSA

½ large cucumber, peeled, deseeded and finely diced
½ red onion, very finely chopped
1 small red (bell) pepper, deseeded and finely diced
2 tbsp red wine vinegar
1 large pinch each of salt and sugar (any type to hand, or use honey)

FOR THE FRITTERS

250g (9oz) courgette (zucchini), coarsely grated (2 small courgettes)
1 large pinch of salt
250g (9oz) raw sweetcorn kernels from 2 smallish cobs
90g (3oz) chickpea (gram) flour
¼ tsp baking powder
1 egg
1 large garlic clove, crushed
½ red onion, very finely chopped
1 large handful of flat-leaf parsley, chopped
salt and freshly ground black pepper
olive oil, for frying

TO SERVE

lemon wedges
a sliced tomato, basil and olive salad
a little extra virgin olive oil

If making the pickled salsa, combine all the ingredients in a bowl and set aside for 20 minutes, stirring now and then.

To make the fritters, turn the oven on low to keep the cooked fritters warm while you finish the batch.

Put the grated courgettes in a bowl and mix the salt through thoroughly. Set aside for 10 minutes. Tip the lot into a clean cloth or tea (dish) towel and wring out over the sink, squeezing very tightly to remove as much excess water as possible.

Add the wrung-out courgettes to the sweetcorn, chickpea flour, baking powder, egg, garlic, onion and parsley in a mixing bowl, seasoning with black pepper and a little salt. Fold together to combine – this makes a thick batter.

Put a large frying pan (skillet) over a medium heat and add about 1½ tablespoons of olive oil. Once the oil is hot, drop in a heaped tablespoon of batter per fritter, to resemble thick Scotch pancakes. You should be able to cook 3–4 at a time, depending on size. Cook for about 2 minutes before flipping them over and cooking for 2 minutes more. They should be golden and set, so turn the heat down a notch if they're browning too quickly. Transfer to paper towels and keep cooked fritters warm in the oven while you cook the remainder in the same way, first adding a little more olive oil to the pan.

Serve the fritters straight away, with the salsa spooned over. A tomato, basil, olive and olive oil salad, plus lemon wedges to squeeze over make excellent accompaniments, as do a few slices of crumbly feta or griddled halloumi.

Summer

Tomato, Crisp Tempeh and Sweet Herb Salad with Macadamias and Lemongrass

Sweet, crisp and perfectly acidic tomatoes make a sumptuous base for a Thai-style salad, fragrant with herbs. Swap the tempeh for extra-firm tofu if it isn't to your taste, or make the salad with strips of omelette instead.

VEGAN
SERVES 4
PREPARATION TIME _____ **25 MINUTES**
COOKING TIME _____ **10 MINUTES**

100g (3½oz) macadamia nuts
2 lemongrass stalks, trimmed and tender parts roughly chopped
2 bird's eye chillies, deseeded if liked
4 shallots, halved
2 fresh lime leaves, very finely shredded
juice of 1 large lime
1 tbsp palm sugar or light soft brown sugar
1 tbsp light soy sauce
200g (7oz) tempeh, sliced 1cm (½in) thick
½ tsp hot smoked paprika
3 tbsp toasted sesame oil
900g (2lb) heirloom tomatoes, sliced or halved according to size
1 handful of Thai basil leaves
1 handful of mint leaves
salt and freshly ground black pepper

Preheat the oven to 190°C (375°F/gas 5).

Spread the macadamias out in a roasting pan and toast in the oven for 8 minutes until they turn a deep golden colour. Cool, then reserve 2 tablespoons and roughly crush the rest.

Make the dressing by roughly chopping 2 shallots and transferring to a pestle and mortar with the lemongrass, chillies and 2 tablespoons of the toasted macadamia nuts. Pound steadily, breaking them down to form a rough paste. Add the sliced lime leaves and pound again to bruise them and release their fragrance. Add the lime juice, sugar and soy sauce. Season to taste with salt and pepper. The dressing should be spiky-hot, sweet, sour and salty, so adjust the sugar, lime juice, salt or chilli levels to suit your taste.

Finely slice the remaining 2 shallots and set aside. Dust the tempeh slices with paprika, season generously and fry in the sesame oil over a medium-high heat for 2–3 minutes on each side until golden and crisp. Tempeh goes sad-looking quite quickly after cooking, so fry it off just before serving the salad.

Gently toss the shallots, prepared tomatoes, hot tempeh and dressing together with the herbs and finish with the reserved, crushed macadamias.

Spicy Tofu-Cashew Satay Bowls with Grilled Asparagus and Edamame

You'll have a generous amount of sauce here and it's all too easy to eat, I'm afraid. Any excess can be used as a dip for summer rolls or raw vegetables, or as a luxurious stir-fry sauce.

Tucked away in this veg-laden recipe is a blueprint for an easy, baked tofu with crisp edges. It will soak up flavours when tumbled into stir-fries or on top of noodle soups.

VEGAN
SERVES 2
PREPARATION TIME _____ 30 MINUTES
COOKING TIME _____ 40 MINUTES

FOR THE SATAY SAUCE

100g (3½oz) unsalted cashew nuts
1 tbsp groundnut (peanut) oil
2 tbsp Vegan Thai Red Curry Paste (see page 217)
　　or use shop-bought
1 tbsp palm sugar or brown sugar
1 tbsp soy sauce
200ml (7fl oz) coconut milk
juice of 1 large lime, plus 1 lime cut into wedges
　　to serve (optional)

FOR THE BOWLS

300g (10½oz) extra-firm tofu, drained and
　　patted dry
1 tbsp toasted sesame oil
1 tsp cornflour (cornstarch)
300g (10½oz) asparagus spears, trimmed
1 tbsp groundnut (peanut) oil
200g (7oz) shelled edamame beans, defrosted
　　if frozen
250g (9oz) cooked brown basmati rice
1 handful of mint leaves
1 handful of Thai basil or coriander (cilantro) leaves
1 small cucumber, sliced
salt and freshly ground black pepper

Preheat the oven to 190°C (375°F/gas 5).

Spread the cashews out in a roasting pan in a single layer and roast for about 9 minutes until golden-brown. Let cool, then roughly crush a third of the nuts and set aside.

Cut the tofu into 2cm (¾in) cubes. Toss with the sesame oil, season with salt and pepper, then dust evenly with the cornflour (a sieve works well for this) and turn to coat. Space out in a roasting pan. Bake for 30 minutes, shuffling the tray every 10 minutes until the tofu is golden and crisp on the outside.

To make the satay sauce, heat the groundnut oil in a frying pan (skillet) set over a low-medium heat and add the red curry paste. Stir-fry for 2–3 minutes until the paste is a couple of shades darker, then add the sugar, soy sauce and coconut milk, stirring until smooth. Simmer down for 1–2 minutes, then transfer to a blender. Add the lime juice and two-thirds of the reserved, toasted cashews. Blend until silken and smooth, adjusting the seasoning to taste. Don't be afraid to add a touch more lime juice, sugar or soy sauce, if needed.

Toss the asparagus spears with the groundnut oil, season and griddle in a smoking-hot pan for about 4 minutes, shuffling around until well-coloured and just tender. They should be charred in places. Add the edamame to the pan and shimmy around for 30 seconds to warm through, then tip the veg onto a plate.

Divide the rice between wide serving bowls and top with the vegetables, herbs, a generous amount of satay sauce, tofu, cucumber and reserved crushed cashews. Offer extra lime wedges alongside, if liked.

This salad is a little unusual, but it works. Soft summer lettuce leaves, avocado, spiced barley and lentils, with a cool, yoghurt-herb dressing and shredded spring onions (scallions). The combination is very loosely based on a Turkish-style, herb, barley and yoghurt soup that I particularly love. Buttery avocado and lettuce leaves and cool slices of cucumber are needed to contrast the grains and dressing. If you want more crunch, add dukkah or toasted seeds right at the end; if you want more peppery notes, add a few radish sprouts or rocket (arugula) leaves. Peeled and halved, soft-boiled eggs are also most welcome.

A note on dried pulses and cooking times: I try to buy dried lentils, beans and so on as I need them, from shops with a high turnover rate. Older pulses that have been stored for a long time definitely take longer to cook, so be aware and prepare to both add an extra splash of water and be more generous with cooking times.

SERVES 4   **AS A SIDE**
PREPARATION TIME   **20 MINUTES**

1 bunch of large salad or spring onions (scallions), dark green tops, shredded and the remainder sliced
20g (¾oz) salted butter
120g (4oz) pearl barley or spelt
90g (3oz) dried brown or green lentils
2 tsp cumin seeds
2 green chillies, deseeded if liked, and chopped
½ tsp ground cinnamon
¾ tsp hot paprika (or add less – this is hot)
500ml (17fl oz) vegetable stock or water
1 small bunch of mint, leaves finely chopped
1 small bunch of flat-leaf parsley, leaves finely chopped
2 tbsp finely chopped chives
finely grated zest and juice of 1 large lemon
2 tbsp Greek yoghurt
1 tsp mild honey
1 garlic clove, crushed
4 tbsp extra virgin olive oil
1 soft (butterhead) lettuce, leaves separated and torn if large
1 large ripe avocado, halved, stoned and diced
1 midi cucumber or ½ large cucumber, peeled and thickly sliced
4 soft-boiled eggs, peeled and halved (optional)
salt and freshly ground black pepper

Start with spiced barley and lentil component; it will sit quite happily for a while after making. In a medium saucepan set over a low heat, soften the sliced whites and pale greens of the spring onions in the butter with a pinch of salt, stirring often. They should be soft, but not coloured after 5 minutes or so. Stir in the barley and lentils with the cumin, chilli, cinnamon and paprika. Cook out for a couple of minutes, frying the grains in the browned butter. Turn the heat up and add the stock (or equivalent water), letting it come up to the boil. Partially cover and simmer over a gentle heat for 25 minutes, or until the lentils are just tender and no liquid remains. Set aside to rest for 5 minutes (small amounts of excess water will be absorbed at this stage), then stir in half the mint, parsley and chives with the lemon zest, check the seasoning levels and set aside. The grain mixture can be served warm or cool.

To make the dressing, whisk the yoghurt, honey, garlic, olive oil and lemon juice together with a generous splash of water to loosen. Season to taste. It shouldn't be a thick vinaigrette – a little thinner in consistency than single cream is ideal.

To construct the salad, put the lettuce leaves on a platter with the avocado and cucumber. Add the remaining mint, parsley and chives with half of the dressing and gently toss together. Scatter with the barley mixture. Spoon the remaining dressing over and strew with the shredded spring onion tops to finish.

Summer

Roast Tomato, Tarragon and Crème Fraîche Tart

Compared to many of the recipes in the book, a buttery puff and cool crème fraîche tart is a more indulgent option, even when generously stacked with the roast tomatoes (masquerading as a magnificent vegetable here, of course). Make the components ahead of time and assemble just before serving with a rocket (arugula) and lentil salad. Alternatively, dispense with the pastry element and serve the roast tomatoes with a grain or pulse (spelt and Puy lentils would be excellent) as a salad, perhaps letting a quarter quantity of the crème fraîche mixture down with a dash of red wine vinegar and plenty of good olive oil to make a dressing. A final thought: double up on the roast tomato quantities, if possible; they make an instant pasta sauce when crushed into their roasting juices and folded through pasta with torn basil.

SERVES 6 — WITH A SIDE SALAD
PREPARATION TIME — 25 MINUTES
COOKING TIME — 1 HOUR 20 MINUTES

FOR THE ROAST TOMATOES

900g (2lb) flavourful, mixed, summer tomatoes
4 garlic cloves, unpeeled and whole
3 tbsp olive oil
1 tbsp fresh thyme leaves
salt and freshly ground black pepper

FOR THE TART

1 egg yolk
1 tbsp milk
a little plain (all-purpose) flour, for dusting
375g (13oz) all-butter puff pastry sheet
2 tsp finely grated fresh horseradish (or 1 tbsp hot horseradish from a jar)
1½ tsp Dijon mustard
1 small bunch of tarragon, finely chopped
300g (10½oz) crème fraîche
salt and freshly ground black pepper

TO SERVE

good-quality extra virgin olive oil

NOTE

Roasting the tomatoes first both concentrates their flavour and ensures their water content won't make the pastry soggy.

Summer

Preheat the oven to 170°C (340°F/gas 3).

Thickly slice the tomatoes if large, halve them if medium-sized and leave whole or on the vine if small. Spread them out in a roasting pan. Tuck in the whole garlic cloves. Drizzle with 2 tablespoons of the oil, scatter with thyme and season with salt and pepper. Roast for 50 minutes or so, depending on their size until the tomatoes are slightly shrivelled and sticky.

Turn the oven to 200°C (400°F/gas 6). Make an egg wash by whisking the egg yolk with the milk in a cup. Unfurl the puff pastry on a lightly floured board and roll out to a 25 x 30cm (10 x 12in) rectangle, trimming the edges straight with a sharp knife. Score a 2.5cm (1in) border around the edge (like a picture frame) with the point of a knife and prick the surface inside the border all over with a fork; this should encourage the strip around the edge to puff up and the middle to stay low as it cooks. Transfer to a large baking (cookie) sheet, brush with the egg wash and bake for 18 minutes or so until the pastry is puffed-up and golden. Set aside.

Squeeze the garlic flesh from the roast cloves into a bowl and crush to a purée with a fork. Stir in the horseradish and mustard with three-quarters of the finely chopped tarragon, then fold in the crème fraîche and season to taste with salt and pepper.

Transfer the tart base to a serving platter or board. Spread thickly with the crème fraîche mixture. Arrange the tomatoes on top in a generous layer. Scatter with the remaining tarragon leaves and drizzle with the remaining tablespoon of olive oil to serve.

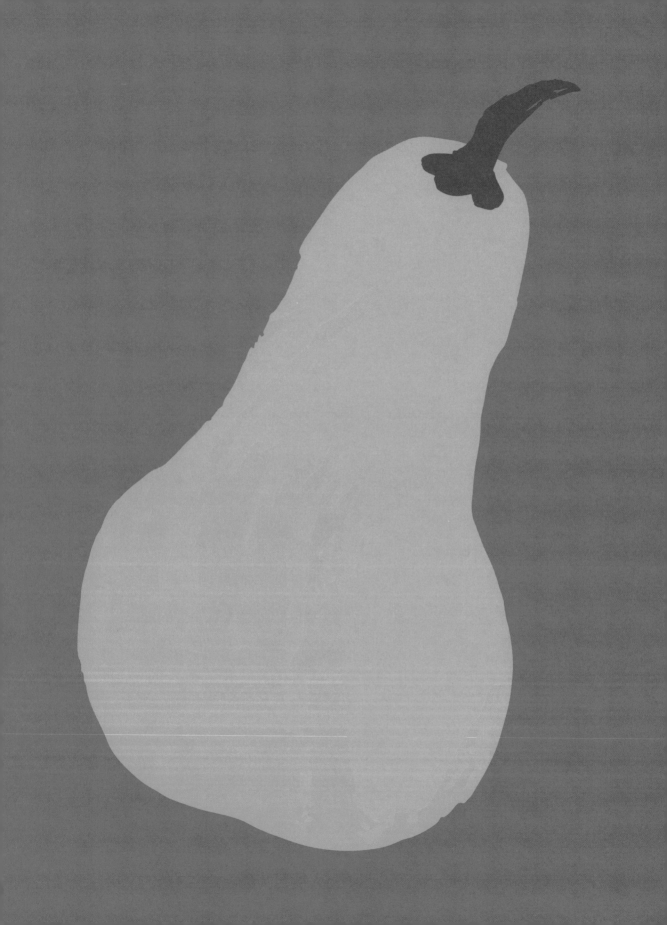

AUTUMN

WHAT'S IN SEASON?

Aubergine

Beetroot

Butternut squash and all pumpkins

Celeriac (celery root)

Chestnuts

Chillies

Cucumber

Fennel

Jerusalem artichokes

Late green beans of all kinds – especially runner

Late sweetcorn

Late tomatoes

Leeks

Maincrop potatoes

Marrows

New season/young nuts

(Bell) peppers

Pulses (fresh and dried)

Truffles

Turnips

Watercress

Wild mushrooms

Autumn

The favourite for cooks, surely? If favourites must be chosen. After the tail end of summer with its most honeyed, ripe, whomps of sweetness, we still we have the corn, gluts of tomatoes and pudgy aubergines. Fruit masquerading as vegetable. Oranges, yellows and reds abound. Then, that mild nip in the dawn air – a question at first – makes way for colder and lengthier snaps until the last of summer has slipped away.

Further riches arrive in the form of pumpkins, winter squash, mushrooms, burly chestnuts, then, too soon afterwards, the first frosts shimmy in to sweeten the earliest roots. That's when our kitchens change once again; back towards soups, stews, curries and comfort. The season of the pulse begins and the year glides surreptitiously on.

Autumn

Spiced Baby Aubergines with Freekeh

Make this as a vegan supper for two, knowing the leftovers will make a superior lunch the next day, with extra salad leaves on the side. It can just as easily be doubled to make supper for a large crowd, perhaps supplemented with falafel, dressed salad leaves, flatbread and hummus to make a mezze-type spread. If baby aubergines (eggplant) – slender or round, it matters not – aren't available, standard, smallish aubergines, quartered lengthways, can be swapped in for every four, as can baby courgettes, like for like.

VEGAN
SERVES 4
PREPARATION TIME _____ 20 MINUTES
COOKING TIME _____ 1 HOUR 10 MINUTES

1 tsp sweet smoked paprika
120ml (4fl oz) extra virgin olive oil
12 baby purple aubergines (eggplant), doesn't matter which shape
8 large shallots, halved
400g (14oz) cherry tomatoes on the vine, snipped into 8 portions using scissors
250g (9oz) uncooked freekeh
400g (14oz) tin of chickpeas (garbanzos), drained
2 garlic cloves, crushed
3 tbsp red wine vinegar
1 tbsp maple or agave syrup
1 tsp ground sumac
2 small bunches of flat-leaf parsley, stalks finely chopped and leaves picked
salt and freshly ground black pepper

Preheat the oven to 180°C (350°F/gas 6). Line a medium roasting pan with baking parchment.

Combine the paprika with 4 tablespoons of the olive oil. Prick the baby aubergines all over with a fork or skewer and put them in the roasting pan with the halved shallots. Drizzle with the spiced oil, turning to coat. Cover with kitchen foil and roast for 45 minutes. Remove the foil, stir and gently nestle the cherry tomatoes in the pan. Roast for about 25 minutes more until the vegetables are well coloured and the tomatoes have begun to split.

Meanwhile, rinse the freekeh in a sieve held under running water. Tip into a saucepan with 650ml (22fl oz) of water and a pinch of salt. Bring to the boil and simmer for 15 minutes until nearly all the water has been absorbed. Add the drained chickpeas to the saucepan for the final 5 minutes so that they heat through thoroughly as the freekeh finishes cooking.

To make the dressing, combine the crushed garlic with the remaining oil, the vinegar, syrup and sumac. Finely chop a small handful of the parsley leaves and stir these in along with the finely chopped stalks. Season to taste.

Gently fold the aubergines, shallots, tomatoes and remaining parsley leaves into the freekeh and chickpea mixture, along with any juices from the roasting pan, spooning the dressing over to finish.

Autumn

NOTE

250g (9oz) raw freekeh makes approximately 500g (1lb 2oz) cooked, in case you need to substitute with a similar cooked grain or rice.

Hot and Sour Vegetable Soup

A winning recipe for when the nights draw in: light, nourishing, comforting and busting with flavour. If you are using easily sourced spring onion (scallion) greens instead of the more elusive garlic chives to finish the soup, add the sliced white parts to the stock at the beginning of the recipe.

VEGAN
SERVES 4
PREPARATION TIME .... 25 MINUTES
COOKING TIME .... 30 MINUTES

1 litre (34fl oz) vegetable stock
30g (1oz) unpeeled galangal or fresh ginger root, sliced
3 lemongrass stalks, bulbs smashed to crush
4 fresh lime leaves, scrunched to bruise
4 Thai or small shallots, unpeeled and halved
4 tbsp tamarind paste
15g (½oz) dried wild or porcini mushrooms (optional but recommended)
2 tbsp light soy sauce
1 large, slender sweet potato, peeled and sliced 1cm (½in) thick
200g (7oz) kohlrabi, peeled and sliced into chubby matchsticks
150g (5oz) shiitake mushrooms, halved if large
8 cherry tomatoes, halved
100g (3½oz) beansprouts
2 tbsp sliced garlic chives or spring onion (scallion) tops
1 small handful of Thai basil, coriander (cilantro) and/or mint leaves, in any combination
salt

TO SERVE
lime wedges
sliced bird's eye chillies

Put the stock, galangal or ginger, lemongrass, lime leaves, shallots, tamarind, dried mushrooms (if using; I'd recommend you do) and soy sauce in a large saucepan. Bring up to simmering point over a medium heat, then turn the heat to low, cover with a lid and let the mixture bubble very gently for 15–20 minutes. Carefully strain to remove the aromatics and return the stock to the pan, seasoning to taste with salt.

Add the sweet potato discs and kohlrabi to the stock. Bring back up to a gentle simmer, letting the liquid blip for about 9 minutes until the vegetables are just tender. Now add the shiitakes and cook for a few minutes more.

Throw in the tomatoes, beansprouts and garlic chives or spring onion greens before removing from the heat. You may want to add a little more salt here. Divide between serving bowls and add the aromatic herbs at the table, along with squeezed lime juice to brighten and eye-watering chilli slices, if liked.

Autumn

Pickled Kohlrabi Salad

What to do with a violet or pale green, Sputnik-shaped kohlrabi? I'd peel it, slice it finely and tumble it into this piquant, Vietnamese-style salad of pickled carrots, sweet pineapple and herbs. The quantities of sweet-sour, *nuoc cham* salad dressing below will make approximately twice as much as you'll need. There comes a point when making less isn't worth it and the dressing has infinite uses as a dipping sauce. Save it for summer rolls, chargrilled vegetables and rice noodle salads, for instance. The pickled carrots need to be made ahead of time and are well worth doubling for similar reasons; they will add to so many salads, wraps and rolls and keep in the fridge for a couple of weeks.

If you can't find kohlrabi or want to make use of a large quantity of broccoli, peeled and finely sliced broccoli stalks make a surprisingly good substitute.

VEGAN
SERVES 4
PREPARATION TIME .... 25 MINUTES
COOKING TIME .... 5 MINUTES

FOR THE PICKLED CARROTS

40g (1½oz) golden caster (superfine) sugar
90ml (3fl oz) rice vinegar
300g (10½oz) carrots, peeled and cut into
   fine matchsticks
salt

FOR THE SALAD DRESSING

4 tbsp golden caster (superfine) sugar
6 tbsp rice wine vinegar
6 tbsp vegan 'fish' sauce or 4 tbsp light soy sauce
juice of 2 limes
2–3 Thai chillies, finely chopped
20g (¾oz) fresh ginger root, peeled and cut into
   very fine matchsticks

FOR THE SALAD

2 tbsp Thai glutinous rice
2 small kohlrabi, peeled and sliced paper-thin
   on a mandoline
200g (7oz) fresh pineapple flesh (prepared weight),
   sliced paper-thin
1 midi cucumber, peeled, if liked, and sliced
1 small bunch of coriander (cilantro), leaves
   roughly chopped
1 small bunch of mint, leaves roughly chopped
1 small bunch of Vietnamese mint or Thai basil,
   leaves picked
50g (1¾oz) cashews, toasted and crushed

Start with the pickled carrots, at least a couple of hours ahead of time. Combine the sugar and vinegar with 50ml (1¾fl oz/3 tablespoons) of water and a pinch of salt in a bowl, stirring until the sugar dissolves. Add the carrot matchsticks and set aside for 2 hours to pickle. The carrots will keep in the fridge in their pickle bath for a couple of weeks.

To make the salad dressing, gently heat the sugar with the vinegar, 'fish' or soy sauce and 120ml (4fl oz) of water until the sugar dissolves. Do not allow the mixture to boil. Let cool. Add the lime juice, finely chopped chillies, depending on your preference for heat, and the ginger.

To toast the rice, put the raw rice in a dry frying pan (skillet) and set over a medium heat. Toast, shuffling and shaking the pan frequently, for about 2 minutes until the rice turns opaque and begins to turn pale golden. Tip into a pestle and mortar and crush to a rough powder. Set aside.

This salad is a cinch to throw together once the components have been prepared and assembled. Toss the kohlrabi, pineapple, cucumber, and 300g (10½oz) of the pickled carrots into a large bowl. Reserve a handful of mixed leaves for garnish and add the rest to the bowl with half of the dressing and half of the cashews. Either serve on a large platter or divide between serving plates, topped with the reserved herb leaves, the remaining cashews and the toasted rice.

Autumn

Baked Tomatoes Stuffed with Antipasti Rice

These handsome fellows are obviously inspired by various Greek, Italian and French ways with rice-filled, slow-baked tomatoes. Cooking tomatoes makes considerably more of the heat-stable antioxidant, lycopene, available to the body so that it can be absorbed. Lycopene has been shown to be beneficial in lowering the risk of some cancer and cardiovascular disease.

Nutrition aside, this is a magnificent way to cook the large, heirloom varieties that are plentiful and relatively cheap in the Northern Hemisphere from July to September. The dish takes a hands-free hour in the oven and will keep in the fridge for a few days, too. I've included gentle hints of saffron and jarred antipasti to the base of wholegrain rice, bolstered with generous amounts of herbs. Dill and oregano are the stars of the herbs here, but you could replace the latter with dried and add or swap in mint or basil for the parsley.

Use any antipasti vegetables you like, in any combination. Stoned olives, sundried or sunblush tomatoes, artichoke hearts or chargrilled vegetables are all ideal. Snip them into olive-sized pieces and also use the oil from the jars or tubs in the recipe.

VEGAN
SERVES 4 _____ **WITH SALAD OR GREEN VEG**
PREPARATION TIME _____ **25 MINUTES**
COOKING TIME _____ **1 HOUR 40 MINUTES**

1 pinch of saffron strands
2 tbsp just-boiled water
1 tbsp olive oil (use the oil from the antipasti jar, if possible)
1 sweet onion, chopped
2 garlic cloves, crushed
250g (9oz) short grain brown rice
1 small glass of dry white wine (optional)
1 litre (34fl oz) vegetable stock
8 large tomatoes (palm-sized and 2.5kg (5lb 10oz) total weight)
300g (10½oz) antipasti in oil, drained (see intro)
30g (1oz) pine nuts, toasted
4 oregano sprigs, leaves stripped and chopped
4 thyme sprigs, leaves stripped and chopped
1 handful of dill, chopped
1 handful of flat-leaf parsley, chopped
a drizzle of extra virgin olive oil or antipasti oil
salt and freshly ground black pepper

Start by making the rice filling. This is essentially a 'lazy' risotto, made with similar ingredients but taking far less care to add the stock gradually, as will become clear. Pour the just-boiled water over the saffron stamens in a small cup and set aside to steep.

Put the tablespoon of oil (from the antipasti or just use olive oil) in a medium saucepan and set over a lowish heat. Add the onion with a good pinch of salt and sizzle gently, stirring often, for 7–8 minutes until softened and translucent, but not coloured. Stir in the garlic and cook for barely a minute, then add the rice and stir to coat. Turn the heat up a touch, slosh in the wine (if using – you don't have to) and simmer until almost evaporated. Now add the stock or water and simmer briskly for 25–30 minutes. Keep a constant eye and stir the mixture often, especially towards the end of the cooking time as it could easily catch as it thickens. By the end, the rice should be somewhere near cooked, but still chalky in texture, and the liquid should be almost gone. Remove from the heat and stir in the steeped saffron mixture. Set aside to cool a little.

Preheat the oven to 170°C (340°F/gas 3).

Have the tomatoes ready on a chopping board with an empty bowl alongside. Ideally using a serrated knife, cut the tops off the tomatoes horizontally. Scoop the exposed insides out with a spoon – such large tomatoes tend to have quite dense innards – and hold

it over the bowl to scrape most of the seeds away. Roughly dice the flesh left behind, discarding any tough inner core.

Stir this diced tomato flesh into the rice with the chopped antipasti, pine nuts and all the herbs. Add a good grinding of black pepper and a little salt, to taste; it should be quite highly seasoned (it's fine to taste-check the mixture, even though the rice will be a little underdone). Drizzle a little oil into a large baking dish, then add the tomatoes. Spoon the

rice filling into them. Be generous. Replace the lids, pressing them down firmly, then drizzle with a little more oil.

Bake the tomatoes for 1 hour until completely tender but still just holding their shape. Serve them warm or at room temperature with any combination of leafy salad, braised greens, lentils or beans, characterful cheese or as part of a barbecue – use your imagination!

Autumn

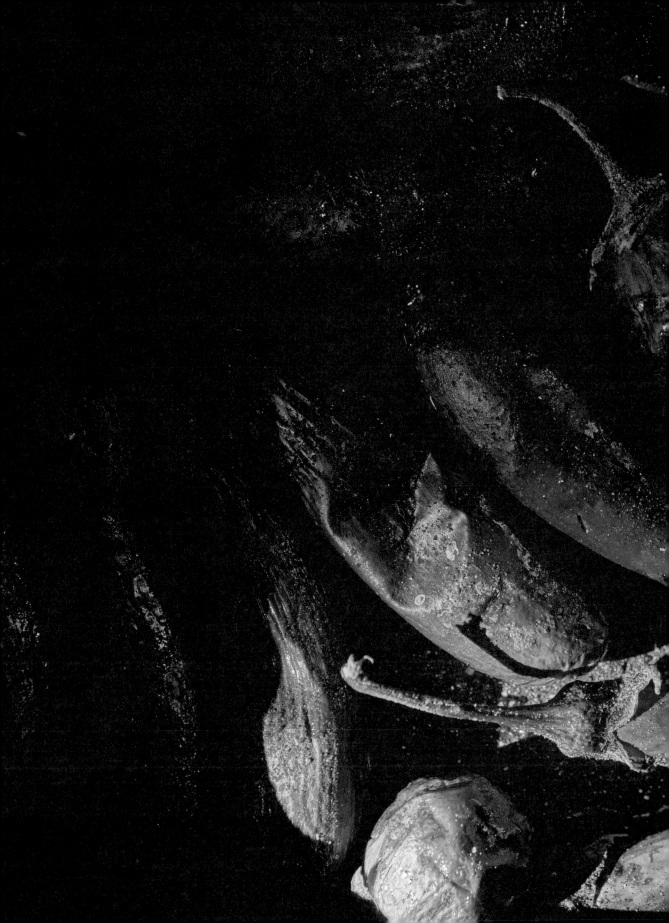

Charred Aubergine Dip
Swirled with Hilbeh

One for early rather than late autumn, before the days get too chilly and when Mediterranean aubergines (eggplant) are still plentiful. This is a recipe for two dips. The former is a brightly spiced herb paste inspired by the Yemeni *hilbeh* – if you've been wondering how to make use of those rock-hard fenugreek seeds in your spice cupboard, this is the one – and the latter a dreamy variation on a *baba ganoush* with whipped, charred aubergine flesh, garlic and tahini. I've left the contents of the vegetable platter open to interpretation so that they can be varied according to what's in season. Think crunchy and fresh to contrast with the dips and pillows of warm flatbread.

VEGAN

SERVES 4	AS A STARTER OR PARTY PLATTER
PREPARATION TIME	30 MINUTES
TO SOAK THE SEEDS	24 HOURS
COOKING TIME	15 MINUTES

FOR THE *HILBEH*

2 tbsp fenugreek seeds
4 plum tomatoes
3 garlic cloves, crushed
1 small bunch of coriander (cilantro) leaves
    and stalks
3 small, hot bird's eye chillies, chopped
1 tsp ground turmeric
½ tsp caraway seeds, toasted
1 tsp cumin seeds, toasted
2 tbsp lemon juice
3 tbsp extra virgin olive oil, plus extra for drizzling

FOR THE SMOKY AUBERGINE DIP

2 large aubergines (eggplant)
100–120ml (3½–4fl oz) extra virgin olive oil,
    as needed
1 tsp cumin seeds, toasted and crushed
4 large garlic cloves, chopped
½ tsp sea salt
150ml (5fl oz) well-stirred light tahini
juice of 2 lemons
salt and freshly ground black pepper

TO SERVE

a rainbow of beautiful, raw vegetables and
    warm strips of flatbread, arranged around
    the dip on a platter

To make the *hilbeh*, you MUST soak the fenugreek seeds in cool water overnight, preferably for up to 24 hours. This will soften them and remove their bitterness. Drain them and transfer to a blender (preferably a bullet-style one).

Cut a shallow cross in the base of each tomato with a sharp knife, place in a heatproof bowl and cover with just-boiled water from the kettle. Leave to steep for 1 minute, then carefully drain away the hot water and peel the skin from the tomatoes, using the scored cross as a starting point. Halve the tomatoes and scoop out the seeds. Add the tomato flesh to the blender with the soaked fenugreek seeds.

Add the remaining ingredients to the blender and blitz to a paste – it needs to be quite fine in texture. Add more oil as needed to keep the blades moving freely. Season to taste, cover and use right away or chill if made up to 24 hours ahead of time.

To make the smoky aubergine dip, turn the grill on as high as it will go. Pierce the aubergines all over with a skewer, coat in 1 tablespoon of the oil and place under the grill for about 15 minutes in total, turning with tongs until blackened all over and soft all the way through. This can also be done over a gas flame, on a barbecue or in the hottest oven. Once cool enough, peel away the charred skin.

Put the warm flesh in a blender with the cumin, garlic, salt, tahini and lemon juice. Blitz to a smooth purée, then gradually drizzle in enough olive oil to make a velvet-textured dip. Taste and adjust the lemon juice or seasoning as needed; though remember the *hilbeh* will alter matters slightly once it's added.

Serve the warm aubergine dip with some of the *hilbeh* spooned over or swirled through (the rest can go in a separate dipping bowl alongside), finished with an extra drizzle of good olive oil.

To serve, make up a beautiful platter with as many raw, seasonal vegetables as you like. Make sure there is lots of colour and crunch from the veg, cut into dippable pieces, and warm flatbreads, torn or sliced.

NOTE

To simplify this recipe, make the smoky, silken aubergine component only and hold back on the *hilbeh*.

Autumn

Candy Beetroot, Bitter Leaf and Halloumi Salad with Fig and Cardamom Dressing

The sweet-sour fig dressing for this exquisite, painterly salad is essentially a fig jam, let down with good olive oil and more vinegar to taste. Double or triple the quantities (but not the star anise) to make more jam for an autumnal cheeseboard or to accompany griddled halloumi, sliced figs and rocket (arugula) leaves in a high-end, toasted sourdough sandwich.

SERVES 4 _____ WITH GOOD-QUALITY BREAD
PREPARATION TIME _____ 30 MINUTES
COOKING TIME _____ 1 HOUR

FOR THE BLACK FIG JAM/DRESSING

1 large, ripe black fig, chopped
1 tsp brown sugar
1 tbsp red wine vinegar
1 star anise
3 green cardamom pods, bruised, seeds removed and crushed

FOR THE SALAD

4 medium, candy-coloured beetroot (beets), scrubbed
3 garlic cloves, unpeeled and whole
6 thyme sprigs
6 tbsp extra virgin olive oil, plus extra to serve
4 tbsp red wine vinegar
1 head red chicory (endive), leaves separated
1 small head radicchio or Treviso, leaves separated
2 x 250g (9oz) blocks of halloumi, drained and sliced 2cm (¾in) thick
about 8 ripest black figs, torn into pieces
salt and freshly ground black pepper

TO SERVE

crusty bread (optional)

To make the black fig jam, which will become the basis of the dressing for the salad, put all the ingredients in a small saucepan set over a medium heat and bring to the boil. Cook down, stirring constantly, for about 6 minutes until jammy and thick, but not burnt. Let cool and remove the star anise.

Preheat the oven to 190°C (375°F/gas 5).

Put the beets on a large sheet of kitchen foil, tuck in the skin-on garlic cloves and 4 thyme sprigs and add 2 tablespoons of the olive oil and 2 tablespoons of the vinegar. Seal tightly to make a parcel, then bake for 45–55 minutes, depending on the size of the beets, until tender to the point of a knife. (No need to unwrap to check this – just go in through the foil.) Once cool enough, peel and slice the beets. Peel and crush the garlic, adding to any liquid in the parcel and set aside to add to the dressing.

Add the fig jam to the beetroot roasting juices with enough of the extra virgin olive oil and the red wine vinegar to make a decadent, sweet-sour dressing, adjusting the salt and pepper levels to taste. If it appears too thick (this will depend on the quantity of beetroot juices), add a generous splash of water to loosen to vinaigrette consistency.

When ready to serve the salad, dry the halloumi slices with paper towel and coat lightly with 1 tablespoon of oil, plenty of black pepper and the leaves from the remaining thyme sprigs. Sear in a smoking-hot, dry frying pan (skillet) until golden on all sides.

Arrange the sliced beets, chicory, radicchio or Treviso, hot halloumi and torn figs on a serving platter. Spoon the dressing over and offer warm, crusty bread to eat with the salad.

Autumn

Roast Butternut, Fennel and White Bean Stew with Bay and Sweet Roast Garlic

This stew is more than the sum of its cosy ingredients, including a sweet fennel base (no onion to be found here, for once). I set out to create a good number of fail-safe, easy and delicious weeknight suppers for the book and this is definitely one of those.

Try soaking the seeds from the butternut squash in heavily salted water for 10 minutes, then drain, toss with olive oil and add to the tray of roasting squash for the final 10 minutes until golden. Scatter the salty, crisp seeds over the stew before eating.

VEGAN
SERVES 4
PREPARATION TIME .... 25 MINUTES
COOKING TIME .... 1 HOUR 20 MINUTES

800g (1b 12oz) peeled butternut squash, cut into
   4cm (1½in) pieces
4 tbsp extra virgin olive oil, or as needed
1 large garlic bulb
1 large fennel bulb, trimmed and quite finely
   chopped, fronds reserved and chopped
8 sundried tomatoes in oil, drained and sliced
1 small glass of dry white wine (about 150ml/5fl oz
   if you're counting)
660g (1lb 7oz) jar of white beans, such as haricot
   or cannellini, with liquor
3 fresh bay leaves, scrunched to bruise
500ml (17fl oz) light vegetable stock
a little lemon juice (optional)
salt and freshly ground black pepper

TO SERVE
good-quality warm bread

Toss the butternut pieces in a good drizzle of oil on a large roasting pan, season and spread out in a single layer. Slice the very top off the garlic bulb horizontally, to just expose the creamy cloves inside. Drizzle with more olive oil and nestle in the middle of the butternut pan. Roast for 40 minutes, or until the squash is caramelized but still holding its shape and the garlic is tender. Squeeze the garlic flesh from the bulb into a bowl and reserve, discarding the papery shell.

Meanwhile, place a medium flameproof casserole or sturdy saucepan over a low heat with a good drizzle of oil in the base. Add the fennel with a pinch of salt and slowly sauté as you would an onion, cooking for at least 10 minutes until translucent and sweet. Add the sundried tomatoes and cook for a further 5 minutes, then turn up the heat and slosh in the wine, stirring. Turn the heat back down once the liquid has disappeared.

Add the beans with their liquor, the reserved roast garlic, bay leaves and stock. Partially cover with a lid and gently simmer for 20 minutes. Remove the lid and bubble down more if the mixture looks soupy. The beans should be extremely tender, creamy and beginning to break down to thicken the stew. Gently add the roast butternut, being careful not to crush it too much, and season to taste. The wine should have added a touch of acidity but consider a squeeze of lemon juice to brighten if you missed it out or can't detect the remnants of a sour bite.

Serve with warm bread, in warmed bowls, scattered with any chopped fennel fronds.

Smoky Aubergine, Rice Noodle and Smoked Nut Salad

More delicious ways with an early autumn hero: charred and shredded aubergine (eggplant) flesh is tumbled with tomato, watercress, rice noodles, armfuls of herbs, edamame and unconventional smoked nuts in this delight of a Vietnamese-inspired salad.

VEGAN
SERVES 4
PREPARATION TIME .... 20 MINUTES
COOKING TIME .... 30 MINUTES

FOR THE SALAD DRESSING

1 small red onion or 2 shallots, halved and sliced
    paper-thin
1–2 tbsp rice wine vinegar, as needed
1 lemongrass stalk, trimmed and finely sliced
1 thumb galangal or fresh ginger root, peeled and
    finely chopped
1 red chilli, finely chopped
1 fat garlic clove, finely chopped
4 tbsp vegan 'fish' sauce
4 tbsp toasted sesame oil
2 tbsp palm sugar or soft brown sugar
juice of 2 limes

FOR THE SALAD

1 extra-large or 2 medium aubergines (eggplant)
1 tbsp olive oil
2 layers of fine, wholewheat rice noodles
2 handfuls of soft herb leaves such as mint
    and coriander (cilantro)
120g (4oz) podded edamame beans, defrosted
    if frozen
150g (5oz) flavourful tomatoes, roughly chopped
    or sliced
50g (1¾oz) (a large handful) tender watercress
    sprigs
50g (1¾oz) smoked macadamia or cashew nuts,
    crushed

To make the dressing, soak the paper-thin slices of red onion or shallot in a bowl of cool water for 10 minutes. Drain and pat dry with paper towel.

Combine all the remaining dressing ingredients with 3 tablespoons of water in a lidded jam jar (use only the single tablespoon of vinegar for now), shake well to mix, then adjust the balance of salty-sour-sweet and hot to taste. You may not need the additional vinegar if your limes were large. Put the onion slices in a bowl with 2 tablespoons of the dressing and set aside for 15 minutes. Reserve the remaining dressing.

Meanwhile, turn the grill on as high as it will go. Pierce the aubergines all over with a skewer, coat in the oil and place under the grill for about 15 minutes in total, turning with tongs until blackened all over and soft all the way through. This can also be done over a gas flame, on a barbecue or in the hottest oven (at a pinch). Once cool enough, peel the charred skin away (this doesn't have to be too precise) and carefully divide the soft flesh into rough strips. Set aside.

Soak the rice noodles in hot water to cook through, according to the packet instructions, then drain. Snip them into slightly shorter lengths with scissors and add to a large bowl with the dressing, soft herbs, marinated onion, aubergine, edamame beans, tomatoes, watercress sprigs and half of the smoked nuts. Gently toss to mix, then divide between serving plates and shower with the remaining smoked nuts.

Corn on the Cob with Mint and Mango Chutney Raita

Something a bit different for fresh corn, assuming that by this time in the season, you'll have had your fill of simply buttered, summer cobs and be ready for adventure. It could be a step too far for some if I were to suggest adding a small amount of crumbled feta or salted Cypriot ricotta to the dressed kernels before eating, but it works if you're that way inclined.

SERVES 4 .... **AS A SIDE**
PREPARATION TIME .... **15 MINUTES**
COOKING TIME .... **30 MINUTES**

4 large corn on the cob, with husks complete
50g (1¾oz) flaked (slivered) almonds
50g (1¾oz) hulled hemp seeds
2 tsp cumin seeds
2 tsp coriander seeds
1½ tsp medium curry powder
½ tsp dried mint
3 tbsp mayonnaise
3 tbsp natural yoghurt
1½ tbsp mango chutney
1 squeeze of lime juice
1 handful of mint leaves, roughly chopped, small
   leaves reserved for garnish
1 handful of coriander (cilantro) leaves, roughly
   chopped, small leaves reserved for garnish
salt and freshly ground black pepper

Preheat the oven to 200°C (400°F/gas 6).

Space the corn cobs out in the hot oven, directly on the middle rack and just as they are, complete with husks and silks and all. Bake for 25 minutes, then remove from the oven using an oven glove, wrap the four cobs in a tea (dish) towel and set aside for 10 minutes to continue cooking in their husks.

Meanwhile, spread the flaked almonds out in a roasting pan and slide into the hot oven for 3 minutes. Scatter with the hemp seeds and return to the oven for 2–3 minutes until the nuts and seeds are lightly toasted.

Toast the cumin and coriander seeds in a dry frying pan (skillet) for a minute or so, adding the curry powder for the final 30 seconds. Crush in a pestle and mortar. Stir half into the toasted almonds and transfer the rest to a mixing bowl. Stir the dried mint, mayo, yoghurt, mango chutney and lime juice into the mixing bowl to make a sauce. Season with a little salt and pepper. Spread the fresh mint and coriander out on a side plate.

Remove the threadlike silks from the corn and peel the husks right back to form a handle. Coat the cobs lightly in the yoghurt mixture, using a spoon to spread it over the kernels. Roll gently in the fresh herbs to coat, then place on a platter. Shower with the nut and seed mixture, followed by the reserved herb leaves.

Fragrant Aubergine, Tomato and Butterbean Curry

There are always standouts when testing and photographing for a cookery book and this is one. It's a stunning recipe with the fresh, balanced and aromatic curry melting into the flesh of a whole roast aubergine (eggplant) per serving. Butter (lima) beans make an inauthentic but welcome addition, soaking up flavours and adding substance. Stir in a couple of handfuls of spinach leaves right at the end if you fancy some extra greenery.

Preparing lemongrass stalks requires removing a lot of the woody outer layers to reveal the more tender, inner core. Instead of composting these tough parts, I freeze them so that I can easily add a handful to plain rice as it simmers, imbuing the grains with a subtle, citrus flavour.

VEGAN
SERVES 4
PREPARATION TIME _____ 35 MINUTES
COOKING TIME _____ 1 HOUR

4 slender aubergines (eggplant),
    about 250g (9oz) each
1 tbsp groundnut (peanut) oil

FOR THE CURRY PASTE

2 lemongrass stalks, trimmed and chopped
2 small shallots, chopped
2 green chillies, chopped (deseeded if liked)
2 thumbs of fresh ginger root, peeled and chopped
1 thumb of turmeric, chopped, or 1 tsp ground
    turmeric
2 large garlic cloves, chopped

FOR THE CURRY

600g (1lb 5oz) ripe, medium-sized tomatoes
1 tbsp coconut oil or groundnut (peanut) oil
1 tbsp palm sugar or light brown sugar
4 lime leaves, scrunched to bruise
2 tbsp tamarind paste
500g (1lb 2oz) cooked butter (lima) beans,
    drained (cooked from scratch or 2 x 400g (14oz)
    tins, drained)
400ml (13fl oz) coconut milk
150ml (5fl oz) vegetable stock
salt and freshly ground black pepper

TO SERVE

plain steamed rice
Thai basil or coriander (cilantro leaves)
lime wedges
sliced chillies

Preheat the oven to 250°C (480°F/gas max) or as high as it will go.

Prick the aubergines all over with a fork, coat lightly with the groundnut oil and place in a roasting pan. Roast for 30 minutes, turning over with tongs halfway through, until blackened and completely soft. Set aside.

Meanwhile, score the bases of the tomatoes with a shallow cross using a sharp knife. Put them in a heatproof bowl and cover with water from a just-boiled kettle. Let steep for a minute or so, then carefully drain away the hot water and peel the skins from the tomatoes, using the cross as a starting point. Roughly chop half of the skinned tomatoes and halve the rest, not worrying about the seeds and pulp; that can all stay, adding flavour.

Blitz the curry paste ingredients together in a mini food processor until quite finely chopped, or use a pestle and mortar to pound everything to a rough paste.

In a flameproof casserole or a large, lidded wok, slowly fry the paste off in the coconut or groundnut oil, keeping the heat quite low so that the aromatics soften and caramelize. Add the sugar and cook out for a minute, followed by the lime leaves, tamarind, butter beans, chopped tomatoes, coconut milk and stock. Simmer for 5 minutes, then add the skinned, halved tomatoes. Cook for a further 15 minutes until the curry has thickened and the halved tomatoes are soft.

Add the roasted aubergines to the curry, first slitting them from top to bottom with a sharp knife to expose their insides. Push down to submerge. Simmer for a few minutes, then remove from the heat and adjust the seasoning to your liking. Consider: does it need more salt,

Autumn

lime juice, palm sugar or perhaps to reduce further and concentrate in flavour? The curry base should be sweet, sour, rich and slightly salty with just a hint of heat, so this is your chance to make it sing, according to your taste.

Serve over plain, steamed rice, scattered with Thai basil or coriander leaves, making the aubergine the star of each serving. If preferred, peel away and discard the blackened aubergine skins as you eat, but they can also be eaten. Offer lime wedges and sliced chillies for squeezing and scattering over, respectively.

Pumpkin and Sweetcorn Soup with Goat's cheese

Chipotle chillies in adobo – widely available in tins or puréed in little jars as a paste – are incredibly useful for adding a smoky bite and depth to naturally sweet, autumnal produce. Here we have a classic trio of pumpkin, late tomatoes and the last of the sweetcorn in a velvet-textured soup. The oven does most of the work for you, caramelizing evenly and saving the bother of sautéing, or even chopping, a base of shallots and garlic.

An obvious point: do use a vegan version of the goat's cheese to keep this soup dairy-free.

SERVES 4
PREPARATION TIME .... 30 MINUTES
COOKING TIME .... 1 HOUR 10–20 MINUTES

1kg (2lb 4oz) dense-fleshed orange pumpkin or winter squash, deseeded, peeled and sliced into 8 long wedges
4 tbsp olive oil
4 small and slender banana shallots, unpeeled and whole
4 garlic cloves, unpeeled and whole
4 rosemary sprigs
100ml (3½fl oz) dry sherry
400g (14oz) plum tomatoes, roughly chopped, or use tinned
1½ tbsp chipotle chilli paste
800ml (28fl oz) vegetable stock
300g (10½oz) sweetcorn kernels, fresh from 2 cobs or frozen
100g (3½oz) soft goat's cheese
1 large red chilli, finely sliced
salt and freshly ground black pepper
1 squeeze of lime or lemon juice (optional)

TO SERVE
1 handful of coriander (cilantro) leaves

Preheat the oven to 190°C (375°F/gas 5).

Toss the pumpkin or squash wedges with 2 tablespoons of the oil, then spread them out in a single layer in a sturdy roasting pan. Make a slit in each shallot with a knife and tuck into the tin. Drizzle a further tablespoon of oil over the top, season with salt and pepper and roast for 25 minutes. Add the garlic and rosemary, shuffling the pan to redistribute, then return to the oven for 20–25 minutes until the squash is soft and caramelized. Discard the rosemary and, when cool enough, peel the shallots and garlic cloves, discarding the skins.

Scrape everything in the roasting pan into a large ovenproof casserole or saucepan and put the roasting pan directly over a medium heat. Add the sherry, using a heatproof spatula to scrape any caramelized bits from the base as it bubbles down. Add the tomatoes and chilli paste and keep stirring. Tip the bubbling mixture into the casserole and place this over the heat. Add the stock and all but a small handful of sweetcorn kernels to the pan, setting these kernels aside. Bring to a simmer. Reduce the heat so that the liquid bubbles gently, cover with an offset lid and leave to simmer for 15–20 minutes.

Blend in the pan with a stick blender, or let the soup cool for 15 minutes before blitzing in an upright blender. Once velvet-smooth, return to the washed-out pan and heat through gently. It shouldn't need it because of the natural acidity of the tomatoes, but when seasoning to taste, consider if the soup needs a squeeze of lime or lemon juice to balance it.

Serve in warmed bowls, topped with the reserved (raw) sweetcorn kernels, sliced chilli, teaspoonfuls of soft goat's cheese and the coriander leaves.

Butternut Puttanesca

This particularly piquant and spicy pasta can handle the extra umami and sweetness that roast cubes of butternut and a generous quantity of sundried tomatoes bring to the sauce. Along with more olives and capers than usual, they make up for the lack of traditional anchovies. No comment on the origin of the title as it's been explained countless times elsewhere – Google it! – this is hardly an authentic version anyway, more of an 'inspired by'. Note that two chillies is very hot while one is a background hum, so only add as required.

VEGAN
SERVES 4
PREPARATION TIME .... 25 MINUTES
COOKING TIME .... 1 HOUR

500g (1lb 2oz) butternut squash, peeled and diced into 2cm (¾in) chunks
3 tbsp olive oil or oil from the sundried tomato jar
3 garlic cloves, finely sliced
1–2 red chillies, sliced, to taste
1 heaped tbsp tomato purée (paste)
100g (3½oz) sundried tomatoes in oil, drained, reserving the oil, and snipped into pieces
400g (14oz) tin of chopped tomatoes
350g (12oz) spaghetti or similar long pasta shape
100g (3½oz) stoned black olives, halved if liked
1 tbsp salted capers, drained and rinsed
1 handful of basil leaves, roughly shredded
salt and freshly ground black pepper

TO SERVE
vegan or vegetarian hard cheese (optional)

Preheat the oven to 200°C (400°F/gas 6).

Toss the butternut squash cubes with 1½ tablespoons of oil in a large roasting pan. Roast for 35–40 minutes until well coloured and sizzling, but still holding their shape. This can be done up to a couple of days in advance and the roast squash kept chilled.

Put the sliced garlic in a cold frying pan (skillet) with the remaining oil and set over a lowish heat. Warm through and allow the garlic to sizzle gently for 1–2 minutes without colouring. Add the chillies, tomato purée and sundried tomatoes, turning the heat up a notch. Stir near-constantly and cook out for a couple of minutes until the tomato purée has separated from the oil. Now add the tinned tomatoes and leave to simmer, stirring occasionally, for 10 minutes. Stir in the roast butternut cubes, olives and capers, warming through for 1–2 minutes.

Meanwhile, cook the pasta in plenty of boiling, salted water for 8 minutes, or according to the packet instructions. When tender, but still with a little bite, drain the pasta in a colander, reserving a small mugful of the cooking water.

Add the pasta to the saucepan, along with a good slosh of hot cooking water, combining with tongs to coat the pasta in the rich sauce. Add more of the starchy water and mix again if it seems too thick. Throw in the basil and season with black pepper (check for salt – it probably won't require much, if any). Divide between serving plates or bowls with extra basil leaves. Shower with grated, hard cheese at the table, if you like, but this richly flavoured sauce doesn't strictly need it.

Autumn

Spiced Roast Squash with Labneh and Crisp Onions

Use any sweet, dense, orange-fleshed winter squash or pumpkin here. Golden butternut will do just fine if you can't find the toad-skinned kabocha or blue-grey crown prince. This makes a stylish side, but you could certainly serve it as a main with a pulse or grain-based salad to accompany.

SERVES 4 — AS A SIDE
PREPARATION TIME — 20 MINUTES
COOKING TIME — 1 HOUR

1 medium kabocha or crown prince squash, halved and deseeded
4 tbsp extra virgin olive oil, plus extra to finish
4 tsp za'atar spice mix
2 tsp thyme leaves
50g (1¾oz) hazelnuts, roughly crushed or chopped
2 large onions, halved and finely sliced
375g (13oz) labneh, goat's curd or very thick, full-fat Greek yoghurt, chilled
1 small handful of flat-leaf parsley leaves
salt and freshly ground black pepper

Preheat the oven to 190°C (375°F/gas 5).

Cut each squash half into 4 even wedges to make 8 wedges in total (no need to peel). Coat the squash with 2 tablespoons of the oil, nestle in a roasting pan, season and roast for about 55 minutes, or until tender and golden. Scatter each wedge with za'atar, thyme and crushed hazelnuts and return to the oven for 5–7 minutes until the nuts are golden.

Meanwhile, put the onions in a frying pan (skillet) with the remaining 2 tablespoons of olive oil and a generous pinch of salt. Place over a lowish heat and cook, stirring often, for 5 minutes until softened. Turn the heat up to medium and continue to cook the onions – they should be sizzling merrily by now – for a further 10 minutes until frazzled, browned and crisp at the edges.

Arrange the squash on a warmed platter, spooning any excess roast hazelnuts and za'atar over with spoonfuls of the labneh (or alternative), the fried onions and the parsley leaves. Drizzle with extra virgin olive oil to finish.

Autumn

Roast Pink Onions and Peppers with Burrata and a Chilli Crumb

A classic idea, re-worked for the autumn months. Indulgent, milky burrata (or mozzarella) is surrounded by sweet roast onions, peppers, crisp sage and a chilli-hot crumb.

SERVES 4	AS A STARTER
PREPARATION TIME	25 MINUTES
COOKING TIME	55 MINUTES

4 pink or red onions, quartered, keeping the root intact
about 7 tbsp extra virgin olive oil
4 tbsp good, aged balsamic vinegar
6 Romano peppers, mixed colours
75g (3oz) sourdough bread, torn or blitzed into small pieces (more like very rough crumbs)
20 small sage leaves: 3 finely chopped and the rest left whole
1 scant tsp dried chilli (hot pepper) flakes
1 garlic clove, crushed
4 burrata or buffalo mozzarella
1 small bunch of purple basil or normal basil, leaves only
salt and freshly ground black pepper

Preheat the oven to 200°C (400°F/gas 6).

Put the onions in a roasting pan with 1½ tablespoons of the olive oil and 1 tablespoon of the balsamic vinegar. Season and cover with kitchen foil. Roast for 40 minutes, then remove the foil and roast for 10 minutes more until soft, sweet and caramelized.

In a separate roasting pan, coat the whole peppers with another ½ tablespoon oil and roast, uncovered, for 30 minutes until soft and charred in places. Tip into a bowl and cover with a plate, then set aside to steam for 10 minutes. Once cool enough, separate the onion quarters a little to create onion petals and peel away the roast pepper skins, discarding any seeds and stalks as you go and tearing the flesh into wide strips. Set aside.

Blitz the torn sourdough in a mini food processor to make rustic crumbs. They don't need to be too uniform; some larger pieces are fine.

Fry the whole sage leaves in a little oil for 1–2 minutes until sizzling but not highly coloured. Set aside on paper towel where they will crisp up as they cool.

Put the chilli flakes, garlic and finely chopped sage in a frying pan (skillet) with 2 more tablespoons of oil. Cook for 1 minute over a medium heat until barely sizzling. Stir in the breadcrumbs and keep cooking until golden. Season with salt and pepper.

To serve, surround each burrata or mozzarella with roasted vegetables. Drizzle with a little more olive oil and the remaining balsamic vinegar, then scatter lightly with the chilli crumbs, the whole fried sage leaves and the basil to finish.

Cajun-Spiced Butternut Squash, Stuffed with Green Rice and Halloumi

Sometimes, a retro vegetarian main course is the winning ticket. This stuffed, baked squash won't win any prizes for modern style, but it is extremely delicious and bursting with flavour, making it ideal for a celebratory supper once the weather has turned. The herb-flecked, spiced-halloumi-studded rice is partly borrowed from a recipe I wrote for Waitrose's *Harvest* column. They've kindly let me reproduce some elements of it here, adding the sweetest roast squash and adapting the rice component to include brown basmati.

SERVES 4 _____ AS A MAIN COURSE WITH SALAD
PREPARATION TIME _____ 30 MINUTES
COOKING TIME _____ 1 HOUR 15 MINUTES

2 small and 'squat' butternut squash (about 1kg/ 2lb 4oz each)
2 tbsp olive oil
4 tsp Cajun spice mix
200g (7oz) brown basmati rice
1 small bunch of flat-leaf parsley, with stalks
1 small bunch of coriander (cilantro), with stalks
¼ tsp salt
4 spring onions (scallions), roughly chopped
2 garlic cloves, roughly chopped
2 green chillies, roughly chopped
230ml (8fl oz) vegetable stock
400g (14oz) tin of black beans, drained and rinsed
2 x 250g (9oz) blocks of halloumi, drained and patted dry
3 limes: juice of 2, 1 cut into wedges
1 large, ripe avocado, halved, stoned and scooped out with a spoon or sliced
salt and freshly ground black pepper

TO SERVE
hot sauce (optional)

Preheat the oven to 190°C (375°F/gas 5).

Cut each squash in half from top to base. Scoop out the seeds with a soup spoon to form four bowls and score the remaining flesh with a knife – about 2cm (¾in) deep – to make a diamond pattern. Coat with ½ tablespoon of olive oil per squash half, making sure the oil gets into the score lines. Season with salt and pepper, then roast for 1 hour until golden and soft. Dust with ½ teaspoon of Cajun spice mix per squash half and roast for 15 minutes more.

Meanwhile, rinse the rice in a colander under cool running water. Drain and transfer to a medium saucepan, uncovered, with 400ml (13fl oz) of water. Bring to the boil, then turn down to a merry simmer for 15 minutes. Set the pan aside, draining off any remaining water, if necessary.

Meanwhile, roughly chop one-third of the parsley and coriander leaves and keep chilled until needed. Add the remaining herbs, including the stalks, to a blender along with ¼ teaspoon of salt, 4 spring onions, the garlic, chillies and 150ml (5fl oz) of water. Whizz to a bright green, finely flecked liquid.

Add the herb liquid and the stock to the rice pan. Bring to the boil, then reduce the heat to a gentle simmer, cover tightly with a lid and leave to cook for 8 minutes. Tip in the black beans, re-cover, and cook for a further 8–9 minutes until tender. Remove from the heat and leave to stand for 10 minutes, still covered, then fluff up the rice with a fork.

While the rice is standing, place a dry frying pan (skillet) over a high heat. Slice the blocks of halloumi into bite-sized cubes. Put the remaining 2 teaspoons of Cajun spice mix on a small plate and toss the halloumi in it to coat evenly. Add the halloumi to the hot pan and cook for 1–2 minutes on each side, turning until highly coloured.

Fold the halloumi through the rice with the lime juice and the reserved chopped herbs. Serve the rice spooned into the bowls of the roasted butternut squash halves. The avocado, doused with a little of the lime and seasoned, can also be folded through or served on the side as a cooling accompaniment along with a green salad.

NOTE

Anoint with hot sauce and extra juice from the lime wedges at the table, if liked.

Autumn

Roast Pumpkin Wedges with Coconut Sambal and Sesame Tofu

Not the only roast winter squash or pumpkin recipe in this chapter, but some seasonal stars deserve to be made a fuss of. I find a generous wedge or two ideal for building a balanced plate of food around, not just for its wow-factor, but because the sweet flesh works so well with a variety of flavours, especially the South East Asian ones celebrated here.

VEGAN
SERVES 4
PREPARATION TIME .... 30 MINUTES
COOKING TIME .... 1 HOUR

FOR THE SAMBAL

3 fresh lime leaves, finely shredded
2 tsp peeled and finely grated galangal or fresh ginger root
scant ½ tsp salt
1 tsp palm sugar or light brown sugar
2 small or 1 large echalion or banana shallots, very finely chopped
2 red chillies, deseeded and finely chopped
90g (3oz) fresh coconut, coarsely grated
juice of ½ lime

FOR THE PUMPKIN AND TOFU

1 small, dense and orange-fleshed pumpkin, cut into quarters and deseeded
3 tbsp groundnut (peanut) oil or mild olive oil
1½ tsp five-spice powder
2 tbsp unsweetened desiccated (dried shredded) coconut
3 tbsp sesame seeds
2 tbsp cornflour (cornstarch)
450g (1lb) block of extra-firm tofu, drained and cut into 2cm (¾in) thick slices
2 tbsp sesame oil
salt and freshly ground black pepper

TO SERVE

1 large handful of watercress or baby spinach

To make the sambal, combine the lime leaves, galangal or ginger, salt and sugar in a pestle and mortar, pounding to break down the lime leaves. Add the shallot and chillies, continuing to break down to make a rough paste (this pounding step isn't strictly necessary, so if you don't have a pestle and mortar, simply combine the finely chopped ingredients, but it will help the flavours to blend properly). Stir in the grated coconut and lime juice. Use straight away or cover and chill for up to 24 hours before serving.

Preheat the oven to 190°C (375°F/gas 5).

Coat the pumpkin or squash wedges with 1 tablespoon of the oil and ½ teaspoon of the five-spice powder in a large roasting pan, seasoning generously with salt and pepper. Roast for 35 minutes until just soft. Scatter half of the desiccated coconut over the pumpkin wedges and return to the oven for 20–25 minutes. By this time, the pumpkin should be caramelized at the edges.

Meanwhile, combine the sesame seeds with the remaining desiccated coconut, the remaining teaspoon of five-spice, the cornflour and a generous seasoning of salt and pepper on a small plate. Lightly dredge the tofu slices in the cornflour mixture, covering the slices as evenly as possible and patting it down to encourage it to stick.

Heat 1 tablespoon of both the sesame and groundnut oils in a large, ovenproof frying pan (skillet) set over a medium heat. Fry half of the tofu slices in a single layer for about 2 minutes on each side, flipping over halfway, until golden. Transfer to a baking tray and repeat with the remaining oil and tofu. Return the first batch of tofu to the pan, trying not to let the slices stick together, then slide them into the oven to bake for 5 minutes or so until golden.

Serve each roast pumpkin wedge with a stack of golden tofu slices, a spoonful of fiery sambal and a handful of spinach or watercress leaves.

Autumn

Carrot and Shallot Tarte Tatin with Fennel Salad

A celebratory, upside-down tart of stubby carrots glazed with a sherry vinegar caramel atop a sautéed mixture of sweet shallots, crunchy fennel seeds and the warmth of dried chilli (hot pepper) flakes. Rather than make a traditional pastry, the crust here is a vegan scone dough of sorts, thrown together in minutes with no need for chilling or resting. Feel free to use a bought or homemade shortcrust, or even a pizza dough in its place.

VEGAN
SERVES 6
PREPARATION TIME .... 40 MINUTES
COOKING TIME .... 1 HOUR 30 MINUTES

about 110ml (3¾fl oz) extra virgin olive oil
400g (14oz) echalion or banana shallots, halved and finely sliced
1kg (2lb 4oz) thick carrots, peeled and sliced into 3cm (1¼in) cylinders
25ml (1½ tbsp) unsweetened plant milk, such as almond or oat
3 tbsp plain vegan yoghurt (soy, oat or coconut) (make sure these are level)
2 tbsp plus 1 tsp mild honey
250g (9oz) wholemeal plain (all-purpose) flour, as needed
2 tsp baking powder
½ tsp fine salt
1 handful of dill, finely chopped
5 tbsp red wine vinegar or sherry vinegar
2 tsp fennel seeds
1 large pinch of dried chilli (hot pepper) flakes (optional)
1 large fennel bulb, trimmed and very finely sliced or shaved, fronds reserved
finely grated zest and juice of 1 lemon
salt and freshly ground black pepper

Put 1 tablespoon of the olive oil in a frying pan (skillet) set over a low heat and add the shallots with a pinch of salt. Cook for 30 minutes, stirring often, until very soft and jammy. Season to taste and set aside.

Meanwhile, cook the carrots in a further tablespoon of oil in a second, large frying pan set over a medium heat. They will take about 15 minutes to brown lightly on all sides. Tip into a bowl and set aside.

Preheat the oven to 190°C (375°F/gas 5).

Combine the plant milk and yoghurt with 1 teaspoon of the honey and 75ml (2½fl oz) of olive oil. Using a palette knife, quickly stir this mixture into the flour, baking powder, salt and 2 tablespoons of chopped dill in a mixing bowl to form a soft, scone-like dough. Add a little extra flour if it seems too wet – this can vary slightly on the day. Roll out between two sheets of non-stick baking parchment to make a circle slightly bigger than the frying pan and slide into the fridge, still in the baking parchment, for 10 minutes.

To make the tart, you'll need a 23cm (9in) diameter, non-stick and ovenproof frying pan. Set it over a medium heat. Add the vinegar and remaining 2 tablespoons of honey with the fennel seeds and the dried chilli flakes, if using. Reduce down for 2–3 minutes to make a syrup without any acrid vinegar smell. Add the carrots to the pan in a tightly packed single layer, sitting as upright cylinders. Continue to bubble down for 3–4 minutes. This will help the carrots to caramelize underneath.

Remove the pan from the heat and carefully cover with shallot jam, spreading it out evenly with the back of a spoon. Unpeel the underside sheet of baking parchment and cover the pan with the scone dough, unpeeling the top layer of paper and quickly tucking the dough in and around at the edges (it will look a bit raggedy; this is fine). Slide it into the middle of the oven.

The tart will take about 50 minutes to cook through; the pastry should be golden-brown on top with the caramel bubbling up at the edges.

Combine the sliced fennel with the lemon zest and juice, a drizzle of extra virgin olive oil, the remaining chopped dill and any chopped fennel fronds saved from the bulbs. Season with salt and pepper.

Remove the tart from the oven and allow it to rest for 5–10 minutes. Cover the pan with the upside-down serving plate (this should have a lip or camber to catch the caramel) and use protective tea (dish) towels to carefully flip the pan and plate over, turning the tart out without scorching your fingers. Top with the crunchy fennel salad, piling it high in the middle, to serve.

Autumn

Roast Celery and Chestnut Soup

Admittedly, this soup isn't much of a looker until anointed with its crisp apple, chestnut and celery leaf topping, but appearances can be deceptive. As is my habit with autumn and winter soups, I like the oven to do the work of caramelizing and concentrating the core ingredients, cutting down on both hands-on cooking time and washing up. Chestnuts, apple and tender roast celery make a subtly sweet, smooth soup, brightened with an essential dash of lemon juice. Consider adding toasted caraway seeds to the base before blending and finishing with a little cream and crumbled blue cheese with the sliced apple to ring the changes (not a vegan variation, obviously).

VEGAN
SERVES 4
PREPARATION TIME _____ 15 MINUTES
COOKING TIME _____ 1 HOUR 20 MINUTES

2 small, crisp eating (dessert) apples
1 small (700g/1lb 9oz) head of celery, rinsed
    and leaves reserved
1 sweet white onion, quartered
4 garlic cloves, unpeeled and whole
3 tbsp extra virgin olive oil, plus extra to serve
2 fresh bay leaves
100ml (3½fl oz) dry white wine or water
900ml (32fl oz) vegetable stock
2 x 180g (6½oz) packs of cooked and peeled
    chestnuts, prepared weight (vacuum packed
    are fine)
3 tbsp lemon juice
salt and freshly ground black pepper

Preheat the oven to 180°C (350°F/gas 4).

Peel, core and roughly slice one apple. Rinse the head of celery to remove any dirt and pat dry. Put it in a large, lidded casserole or heavy-based saucepan (if the celery is too long to fit in, lop it in half) with the sliced apple. Add the onion quarters, oil and bay leaves. Add the white wine or water. Cover with a lid and bake in the middle of the oven for 1 hour until the celery is very tender and caramelized. Carefully remove the garlic skins, returning the garlic to the pot with the stock and all but 4 of the cooked chestnuts. Put back in the oven, covered, for 20 minutes more.

Remove the bay leaves and either purée the mixture in the pot with a stick blender, or let cool for 15 minutes and blitz in an upright blender, in batches, until velvet-smooth (too hot and the liquid will create a vacuum). Return to the original pot and add 2 tablespoons of the lemon juice, followed by salt and pepper to taste.

Cut the remaining apple into fine matchsticks, discarding the core. Slice the reserved chestnuts and combine with the celery leaves, apple, remaining tablespoon of lemon juice and a dash of olive oil.

Gently reheat the soup when needed and serve in warmed bowls, topped with the crisp apple salad and an extra drizzle of peppery olive oil.

Autumn

Tomato and Lentil Cornbread

Make this handsome, autumnal or late summer cornbread ahead of time and you've got a hearty base for a weekend brunch or breakfast. Top warm squares of it with any combination of poached or fried eggs, avocado, hot sauce and extra tomatoes. You'll notice I've thrown unconventional red lentils into the batter to add a little extra protein, character and texture, cooked through before stirring in. Feel free to replace them and their cooking step with an extra 100g (3½oz) raw cornmeal or polenta to simplify the method.

SERVES 8
PREPARATION TIME .... 30 MINUTES
COOKING TIME .... 1 HOUR 10 MINUTES

3 tbsp oil (either use olive or oil from the sundried tomato jar)
8 oregano sprigs
100g (3½oz) red lentils, rinsed in a sieve
350g (12oz) coarse cornmeal or polenta
1½ tsp baking powder
½ tsp bicarbonate of soda (baking soda)
½ tsp sea salt flakes
2 large eggs
300g (10½oz) Greek yoghurt
150ml (5fl oz) milk
200g (7oz) sundried tomatoes in oil (drained weight)
400g (14oz) mixed cherry tomatoes, on the vine if liked
1 large red chilli, sliced
1 small red onion, finely sliced into rings
2 sweetcorn cobs, kernels sliced off

Preheat the oven to 180°C (350°F/gas 4). Use 1 tablespoon of the oil to grease a 23cm (9in) diameter cast iron or sturdy ovenproof frying pan (skillet) or a 20cm (8in) square oven dish or pan.

Strip the oregano leaves from 2 sprigs and set aside. Put the red lentils in a small pan with 250ml (8½fl oz) of water. Bring to the boil, cover with a lid and simmer for 15 minutes, stirring occasionally, until the lentils are soft and the water has been absorbed. Set aside to cool for at least 10 minutes.

Combine the cornmeal or polenta, baking powder, bicarbonate of soda and salt in a large mixing bowl. Add the lentils, eggs, yoghurt, milk and sundried tomatoes, combine lightly, then spoon into the dish or pan.

Gently press a jumble of the remaining oregano sprigs, tomatoes (still on the vine if that's how they come), sliced chilli, sliced red onion and sweetcorn kernels over the top, distributing everything as evenly as possible. Drizzle with the remaining 2 tablespoons of oil. Bake for about 55 minutes, or until well risen and firm in the middle with a good, golden colour and darker edges. Check after 30 minutes and cover loosely with a sheet of kitchen foil with a small circle in the middle torn out (to allow the steam to escape) if the cornbread is browning too quickly. This will allow it to cook through in the middle while not over-browning elsewhere.

Remove the dish from the oven and set aside to rest for at least 15 minutes before slicing the cornbread into generous pieces. Serve warm with any combination of poached eggs, hot sauce, avocado and extra tomatoes, if liked.

Autumn

Harissa, Butterbean and Aubergine Patties with Confit Aubergine and Peppers

Characterful, pulse-based patties, falafels, burgers and balls are endlessly useful in any vegetarian kitchen. You'll find a few variations throughout this book because they're a winning stand-by, combined with seasonal vegetables and interesting sauces or dressings. The possibilities are endless, but the harissa, silken aubergine (eggplant), tahini, butter (lima) beans, salted yoghurt and confit veg used here make a dream combination for October or November cooking. Make the patty mixture in advance if you want a much quicker supper on-hand. It will keep in the fridge for at least 48 hours before cooking.

SERVES 4   MAKES 20 PATTIES
PREPARATION TIME   30 MINUTES
COOKING TIME   1 HOUR 30 MINUTES

FOR THE AUBERGINE AND BUTTERBEAN PATTIES

1 large, sweet onion, finely chopped
2 tbsp olive oil
2 large aubergines (eggplant), cut into
   2cm (¾in) cubes
2 tbsp harissa paste
2 garlic cloves, crushed
2 x 400g (14oz) tins of butter (lima) beans, rinsed
   and drained
2 tbsp well-stirred tahini, plus extra to serve
   (optional)
50g (1¾oz) dried or very stale breadcrumbs
1 handful of basil and coriander (cilantro) leaves,
   finely chopped, plus extra basil leaves to serve
90g (3oz) walnuts, toasted and roughly crushed
   or chopped
salt and freshly ground black pepper

FOR THE CONFIT AUBERGINE AND PEPPERS

3 bay leaves, fresh or dried
3 tbsp extra virgin olive oil
1 tbsp harissa paste
2 aubergines (eggplants), each sliced into
   8 long wedges
2 large Romano peppers, deseeded and
   quartered lengthways
juice of ½ lemon
salt and freshly ground black pepper

TO SERVE

450g (1lb) strained Greek yoghurt
lemon wedges, if liked

NOTE

You can make the mixture 48 hours in advance
and keep chilled.

Preheat the oven to 180°C (350°F/gas 4).

To make the confit aubergine and peppers, put the bay leaves, olive oil, harissa and 3 tablespoons of water in a medium baking pan. Add the veg and season with salt and pepper. Cover tightly with kitchen foil and bake for 50 minutes, checking halfway and adding a further splash of water if the vegetables are catching too much. Stir gently, then remove the foil and cook for 15 minutes more until the vegetables are very soft and beginning to brown. Remove from the oven and add the lemon juice.

To make the patties, soften the onion in 1 tablespoon of the olive oil for 5 minutes over a lowish heat. Add the aubergines with a pinch of salt and cook gently, stirring, for 15 minutes until soft and turning golden. Stir in the harissa paste and turn up the heat a little. Sizzle down for 5 minutes, then add the garlic for a final minute and remove from the heat.

Ideally using a large pestle and mortar, roughly crush the drained butterbeans. The tines of a fork will also do, or a food processor will get the job done. Transfer to a mixing bowl with the tahini, breadcrumbs, chopped herbs, 50g (1¾oz) of the walnuts and the onion-aubergine mixture. Season well with salt and pepper and fold together.

Increase the oven to 190°C (375°F/gas 5). Form the patty mixture into large, walnut-sized rounds with oiled hands (using the remaining tablespoon of olive oil). Space out on lined baking trays and bake for about 25 minutes until browned.

Season the yoghurt with a little salt and spoon onto serving plates or a platter. Top with the confit peppers and aubergine (these can be at room temperature), the patties and a few more basil leaves, adding the remaining walnuts and an extra drizzle of tahini, if liked.

Autumn

WINTER

WHAT'S IN SEASON?

Beetroot (beets)

Brussels sprouts

Cauliflower

Celeriac (celery root)

Celery

Chicories and endive

Horseradish

Kale

Kohlrabi

Leeks

Mushrooms

Parsnips

Potatoes

Pulses (dried)

Winter

It's properly chilly now, rather than just dull or damp. While not vegetables, citrus and pomegranate have arrived to assist, adding vibrant colour and acerbic juice to contrast candied, baked roots and squash. Celebrations revolve around the kitchen and, where Christmas is concerned, around endless vegetable sides. This is the fun bit; the cosy, generous bit. Followed afterwards by the inevitable re-set of crunch and colour; brassicas being slivered into slaws rather than gratins and dark leafy greens by the armful. The challenge comes at the end, when winter almost becomes spring again – too late for the sweetest parsnips, too early for the crunch of new radishes. Hold on tight with the kales, the broccolis and the mature, knobbled roots until it's time for the spring to gently bloom once again.

Parsnip Falafel with Pomegranate and Tahini

It turns out quite a traditional falafel mixture can take a judicious amount of raw, grated parsnip in the mix, making it naturally sweeter and nuttier. As with any falafel made with soaked chickpeas (garbanzos), you will need a good food processor to get the correct consistency of batter, meaning the patties won't break up on frying. Other tricks for success include adding a little chickpea or gram flour to the mix and being very firm when shaping the falafel. If in doubt, freeze them on open trays for an hour, once shaped. I've cheated here with bought parsnip crisps to add crunch to the platter; feel free to fry your own ribbons or swap in sticky, roast wedges of parsnip. If you don't like the fabulous flavour of dill, these falafel won't be for you as written, so swap out the dill for more flat-leaf parsley and/or coriander (cilantro) or basil.

Note that this recipe requires you to soak dried chickpeas (garbanzos) in water for a minimum of 12 hours or up to 24 hours ahead of time.

VEGAN

SERVES 4	MAKES 20 FALAFEL
PREPARATION TIME	40 MINUTES
TO SOAK THE CHICKPEAS	12–24 HOURS
COOKING TIME	10 MINUTES

300g (10½oz) dried chickpeas (garbanzos)
1 tsp fennel seeds
1½ tsp cumin seeds
1½ tsp coriander seeds
200g (7oz) parsnips, peeled and coarsely grated
1 small red onion, roughly chopped
4 garlic cloves, crushed
1 tsp fine salt
4 tbsp chickpea (gram) flour
¾ tsp bicarbonate of soda
2 small bunches of dill, roughly chopped, plus extra
    leaves to serve
1 small bunch of flat-leaf parsley, roughly chopped,
    plus extra leaves to serve
1.5 litres (52fl oz) vegetable or sunflower oil,
    for frying
2 lemons: 1 juiced, the other cut into wedges
4 heaped tbsp well-stirred tahini
4 tbsp pomegranate molasses
1 small pomegranate, arils only
salt and freshly ground black pepper

TO SERVE
75g (2½oz) parsnip crisps
100g (3½oz) baby spinach leaves

Start by putting the dried chickpeas in a large bowl and covering generously with cold water. They will swell up considerably, so leave room at the top. Set aside to soak in a cool room for a minimum of 12 hours or up to 24 hours. I've been known to leave them for 48 hours, changing the water a couple of times.

When ready to make the falafel batter (which can also be made a couple of days ahead of time and kept covered and chilled, as can the shaped falafel), preheat the oven to its lowest setting.

Put the fennel, cumin and coriander seeds in a cold, dry frying pan (skillet) and place over a medium heat. Shimmy the pan around as the seeds warm through, toasting them for 1–2 minutes until fragrant and a shade or two darker. Tip into a pestle and mortar to crush or grind down on a chopping board with the base of a sturdy jar.

Put the ground spices in a food processor fitted with a sharp blade (not a blender – that won't work here) and add the well-drained chickpeas, grated parsnip, red onion, 3½ of the crushed garlic cloves and the salt to the bowl. Blend, stopping to scrape down the sides every now and then, until the ingredients are very finely and evenly chopped. Add the chickpea or gram flour and the bicarbonate of soda. Blend again until the mixture begins to clump together and form a paste. Lastly, add the dill and parsley, pulsing until the herbs are finely chopped. Scrape into a lidded container and chill the mixture for at least 30 minutes.

Winter

With clean hands, form the chilled mixture into about 20 round discs, pressing the mixture together firmly. This will help the falafel to hold steady when frying. Space out on a lined baking tray.

Put the oil in a deep-sided saucepan, it should sit about 5cm (2in) deep. Place the pan over a medium heat and let the oil come up to temperature slowly. It should be at 180°C (350°F) on a thermometer or turn a cube of white bread golden in 30 seconds. Carefully add about one-third or even half of the falafel to the pan, lowering them in on a slotted spoon, one by one. Fry for 4–5 minutes,

turning often until golden. Remove to a plate lined with paper towel using the slotted spoon, then transfer to the oven to keep warm. Repeat with the remaining falafel.

Stir the lemon juice and remaining ½ clove of crushed garlic into the tahini with salt and pepper and 3–4 tablespoons warm water, to make a thick sauce.

Serve the hot falafel over spoonfuls of this tahini sauce, drizzled with pomegranate molasses and scattered with pomegranate arils. Accompany with the parsnip crisps, spinach leaves, extra dill and parsley sprigs and lemon wedges to squeeze over.

Winter

Popcorn Cauliflower

This fragrant, popcorn cauliflower, served with sticky sweet chilli, is a delight – and vegan, too. Feel free to deep-fry the dredged florets in hot oil for 5 minutes if you prefer; you'll need a couple of litres of oil to cook this much in batches. The oven-roasted method below gives excellent results for far less oil and wins out over frying for me. This feels like party starter or snack territory, but could certainly make a main for two or three diners, served with the chilli jam, rice, greens and perhaps some tofu or a fried egg (the latter for the non-vegans).

VEGAN
SERVES 4 _____ AS A SNACK OR SIDE
PREPARATION TIME _____ 15 MINUTES
COOKING TIME _____ 30 MINUTES

1kg (2lb 4oz) cauliflower (1 large), trimmed
400ml (13fl oz) coconut milk
4 tbsp soy sauce
4 lime leaves, finely shredded or chopped
2 lemongrass stalks, trimmed and finely chopped
125g (4oz) cornflour (cornstarch)
200g (7oz) plain (all-purpose) flour
5 tbsp groundnut (peanut) oil
2 red chillies, finely sliced into rounds
1 large thumb of fresh ginger root, peeled and sliced into matchsticks
1 small bunch of Thai basil leaves
salt and freshly ground black pepper

TO SERVE
lime wedges
sweet chilli jam

Break or slice the cauliflower into bite-sized florets. Put these florets in a mixing bowl with the coconut milk and soy sauce. Leave for 20 minutes minimum, or for up to 24 hours in the fridge, stirring regularly.

Preheat the oven to 200°C (400°F/gas 6). Have two large roasting pans ready, lined with non-stick baking parchment.

Combine the flours in one mixing bowl with the lime leaves and lemongrass. Season generously with salt and pepper, then transfer half of this mixture to a second mixing bowl. This is to stop the flour getting too 'gummy' when dredging the florets. Drain a handful of cauliflower florets above their soaking bowl and lightly toss with the flour in one bowl, jumbling them around so that it sticks evenly, and shaking off the excess. Space out in the pans and repeat to use up all of the remaining florets, moving to the next bowl of seasoned flour once the first one becomes too sparse and claggy.

This is a time when an oil spritzer would come in useful to spray the florets with a light coating of oil. Otherwise, just drizzle them evenly with 4 tablespoons of the oil and toss very gently to coat. Bake both trays of florets for 25 minutes, giving the pans an energetic shake and shuffle halfway through to redistribute the oil and cook out all the flour in the coating.

Meanwhile, place the remaining tablespoon of oil in a cold frying pan (skillet) and add the red chillies and ginger. Set over a medium heat and fry, stirring often, for about 3 minutes until sizzling and frazzled. Scatter over the baked cauliflower with the Thai basil leaves and serve with the chilli jam and lime wedges, for dipping and dousing.

Winter

Hasselback Celeriac Parcels with Winter Herbs

A slow-roast celeriac (celery root) turns magically sweet, nutty and almost translucent in the oven, absorbing just enough flavour from the winter herbs. Half of one of these buttery vegetables, scored like a hedgehog to scent with herbs, would make a centrepiece to a vegetarian Sunday roast, or a wintery side to any number of stews or lentil braises, lavished with spoonfuls of Salsa Verde (see page 219).

SERVES 4 _____ AS A SIDE OR 2 AS A MAIN
PREPARATION TIME _____ 15 MINUTES
COOKING TIME _____ 1 HOUR 45 MINUTES

2 x 720g (1lb 9½oz) celeriac (celery root)
4 small rosemary sprigs
6 small thyme sprigs
4 bay leaves
50g (1¾oz) butter, softened, or 3 tbsp olive oil
150ml (5fl oz) dry white wine
salt and freshly ground black pepper

Preheat the oven to 200°C (400°F/gas 6).

Pare all the knobbly bits and skin from the celeriac to reveal two creamy white and green orbs. Carefully make vertical cuts in each, reaching two-thirds down the vegetable, spaced about 5mm (¼in) apart. Sit each in the middle of a square of baking parchment, stick the herb sprigs and leaves into the cuts randomly. Spread the top of each celeriac with half of the butter (or use olive oil instead), season with salt and pepper and carefully pour in half the wine with 2 tablespoons of water, bringing the paper up and around the celeriac to wrap. Use kitchen string to secure the parcel – like a panettone or one end of a cracker – at the top.

Repeat with the second celeriac and roast side by side for about 1 hour 45 minutes, carefully swirling or turning the parcels around at a couple of points, using oven gloves, to baste the vegetables in the butter and wine; otherwise it just collects at the base. At the end of their cooking time, the celeriac should be completely tender to the point of a knife and turning golden. Open the parcels at the table to serve.

Winter

Ginger-Miso Sweet Potato Wedges

A favourite for parties in various guises, these wedges are baked with an umami-heavy, sticky glaze that bubbles down to form the most delicious lacy edges and crunchy corners. It is served with a wasabi mayonnaise in which to cloak them. Scatter the wedges with sliced chilli, shaved radish slices and purple radish sprouts if you'd like to pretty them up for serving, but they don't need it.

SERVES 4	AS A SIDE
PREPARATION TIME	25 MINUTES
COOKING TIME	1 HOUR

800g (1lb 12oz) (4 medium) sweet potatoes, scrubbed and each sliced into 8–10 wedges
3 tbsp groundnut (peanut) oil
2 tbsp mirin
1 tbsp finely grated fresh ginger root
1½ tbsp white miso paste
1 tbsp maple syrup
1 tbsp sesame oil
2 tbsp light soy sauce
1 tbsp wasabi paste
4 heaped tbsp Japanese mayonnaise
2 tbsp lime juice
salt

Preheat the oven to 200°C (400°F/gas 6).

Toss the sweet potatoes with the oil and spread out in a single layer in a roasting pan. Cook for about 30 minutes until just beginning to colour.

Combine the mirin, ginger, miso, maple syrup, sesame oil and soy sauce in a bowl. Season with a little salt. Drizzle this mixture evenly over the partially cooked sweet potatoes and return to the oven for 20 minutes or so, carefully turning over once or twice until they are well caramelized.

Mix together the wasabi, mayonnaise and lime juice and serve with the wedges.

Winter

Roast Sweet Potatoes
with Sesame, Yoghurt and Harissa

You could really gild the lily here by adding spiced, roasted chickpeas (garbanzos) to an already lavish mix of flavours, but these roast potatoes are quite wonderful as they are, with layer upon layer of sweet and savoury flavour and texture. They only need a peppery salad or wilted greens to make the perfect meal.

SERVES 4 AS A SIDE OR AS A MAIN WITH SALAD
PREPARATION TIME _____ 20 MINUTES
COOKING TIME _____ 1 HOUR 30 MINUTES

4 large, slender sweet potatoes, scrubbed
    (about 300g/10½oz each)
2 tbsp olive oil
3 red onions, halved and finely sliced
1 pinch of sugar (optional)
1 tsp cumin seeds, toasted and roughly crushed
1 garlic clove, crushed
3 tbsp well-stirred brown or light tahini
finely grated zest and juice of 1 large lemon
4 heaped tbsp Greek yoghurt
2 tbsp rose harissa paste
1 small bunch of coriander (cilantro), leaves only
2 tsp toasted black sesame seeds
salt and freshly ground black pepper

Preheat the oven to 200°C (400°F/gas 6).

Prick the sweet potatoes with a sharp knife. Space them out in a roasting pan and bake for 1 hour until completely tender.

Meanwhile, put the oil in a medium saucepan set over a low-medium heat and add the onions with a pinch of salt. Cook slowly, stirring often, for 25–30 minutes until very soft and caramelized. You can add a pinch of sugar after 20 minutes to encourage the process along, if you like. Stir in the cumin, season to taste with salt and pepper and set aside.

In a small bowl, combine the crushed garlic clove with the tahini, lemon juice and 40–60ml 1½–2 tbsp warm water, as needed (add enough to make a sauce with the consistency of double cream). Season with salt and pepper.

Season the yoghurt with salt and partially swirl the harissa through it in a bowl.

Split the cooked sweet potatoes open and fill haphazardly with spoonfuls of the harissa yoghurt, coriander leaves, the tahini sauce, caramelized onions and black sesame seeds. Sprinkle the lemon zest over to finish.

Winter

Parsnip, Brussels and Nutmeg Rigatoni Gratin

A more indulgent recipe than I habitually write; I don't typically use a lot of rich cream or dairy-based sauces, preferring the clout of chilli, citrus, flavourful oils and dressings, fresh herbs, toasted nuts and the like to the sometimes cloying richness of a cheese sauce. But this is a nod to Christmas and with Christmas come the rich exceptions.

SERVES 6 .... **AS A SIDE**
PREPARATION TIME .... **30 MINUTES**
COOKING TIME .... **1 HOUR 30 MINUTES**

500g (1lb 2oz) slender parsnips
1½ tbsp olive oil
200g (7oz) dried rigatoni, penne or similar short pasta tubes
200g (7oz) raw Brussels sprouts, trimmed and sliced
450ml (15¾fl oz) whole milk
2 fat garlic cloves, bruised
3 bay leaves, bruised
7 thyme sprigs
1½ tsp freshly grated nutmeg
30g (1oz) butter
30g (1oz) spelt flour or plain (all-purpose) flour
200ml (7fl oz) crème fraîche
250g (9oz) Gruyère coarsely grated
3 tbsp finely grated, vegetarian parmesan-style cheese
90g (3oz) walnuts, roughly crushed
salt and freshly ground black pepper

Preheat the oven to 180°C (350°F/gas 4).

Top, tail and peel the parsnips and reserve the peelings and trimmings. Cut the parsnips into thumb-sized pieces or slices and toss with the oil. Spread out in a roasting pan in a single layer, season with salt and pepper and roast for 35–40 minutes, shimmying halfway through until just tender and turning golden.

Meanwhile, cook the pasta in a large saucepan of plenty of boiling salted water for 3 minutes, then add the sliced Brussels sprouts and simmer for a further 2 minutes. Drain in a colander, refreshing very briefly under cool water. Put the milk in the same (empty) pasta pan with the bruised garlic and bay, 4 of the thyme sprigs and 1 teaspoon of the nutmeg. Add the parsnip peelings and simmer gently for 10 minutes, then remove from the heat, cover and leave to sit for 15 minutes. Strain the flavoured milk into a jug.

Rinse out the pan and return it to a lowish heat with the butter and flour, stirring with a wooden spoon to make a paste. Cook this out for 4–5 minutes, really toasting the flour and letting it fizz. Now scrape the roux to one side of the pan and slosh about 150ml (5fl oz) of the infused milk into the empty part of the pan, allowing it to heat through slightly before briskly whipping it into the roux with a balloon whisk. Letting the milk heat through first will help prevent lumps forming. Keep going in this way, adding the milk, but giving it a moment to warm through before whisking in, until it has all been incorporated. Now whisk in the crème fraîche and bring the mixture to a gentle boil. Simmer this rich sauce, stirring, for 5 minutes to cook out every remnant of flour taste, then remove from the heat and add the cheeses with the remaining ½ teaspoon of grated nutmeg. Leave for 2 minutes, then stir well and season to taste.

Add the pasta, sprouts and roast parsnips to the sauce, folding everything together. The melted Gruyère cheese will have made its elasticated presence known by this point. Spoon into a 20 x 30cm (8 x 12in) baking dish and top with the leaves from the remaining 3 thyme sprigs and the crushed walnuts.

Bake the gratin in the oven for about 25 minutes until the nuts are golden and the edges bubbling.

Blistered Tomato Confit on a Parsnip Rosti with Capers and Oregano

It's the contrasts that make a great vegetarian dish. This crisp-edged rosti with a tender middle is topped with syrupy-soft, confit tomatoes in vinegar, salt-bomb capers and the hum of oregano (substitute thyme, if you like). I didn't add it for the picture, preferring the vibrant, minimal look, but a cold spoonful of crème fraîche, added to the sizzling rosti, will melt into the confit tomatoes quite beautifully.

SERVES 2–3
PREPARATION TIME _____ 25 MINUTES
COOKING TIME _____ 45 MINUTES

6 tbsp olive oil
1 small onion, finely chopped
2 tsp thyme leaves
250g (9oz) parsnips, trimmed and scrubbed
250g (9oz) baking potatoes, scrubbed
1 squeeze of lemon juice
2 tsp cornflour (cornstarch)
    or plain (all-purpose) flour
20g (¾oz) unsalted butter
1 tbsp capers, rinsed and dried
2 garlic cloves, finely sliced
200g (7oz) cherry tomatoes, mixed colours
    if possible
1 tsp marjoram or oregano leaves
2 tbsp red wine vinegar
2 tbsp crème fraîche (optional)
salt and freshly ground black pepper

Preheat the oven to 200°C (400°F/gas 6).

Put 1 tablespoon of the olive oil in a 20cm (8in) non-stick, ovenproof frying pan (skillet) and set over a medium heat. Add the chopped onion and a pinch of salt and sauté for 7–8 minutes. Stir in the thyme leaves and tip into a bowl.

Coarsely grate the parsnips and potato, then toss with the lemon juice. Tip into a clean tea (dish) towel and firmly squeeze out over a sink to remove any excess water from the potatoes. Tip into a bowl and add the sautéed onion and cornflour, then season.

Wipe out the frying pan. Put 2 tablespoons of the olive oil and the butter in the pan and place over a high heat for 30 seconds. Spoon the rosti mixture in (it should sizzle), flattening it down firmly, especially around the edges. Turn the heat down to low-medium and cook for 10 minutes, releasing the edges with a spatula once they look golden. Using a tea towel to protect your hands, place an upside-down plate over the pan, then flip the lot to turn the rosti out. Add another 1 tablespoon of olive oil to the pan and slide the rosti back in. Return to the heat for 10 minutes, then put the pan into the oven for a further 10 minutes until the rosti is deeply browned and sizzling. Keep warm.

Put the remaining 2 tablespoons of oil in a separate frying pan set over a medium heat and add the capers. Cook, stirring, for a couple of minutes until crisping up, then throw in the sliced garlic and cherry tomatoes. Continue to cook, turning the heat up a notch, for a few minutes until the tomatoes begin to catch and burst. Add the marjoram or oregano, followed by the red wine vinegar. Bubble down for a minute, then season well with salt and pepper.

Carefully flip the rosti onto a chopping board or serving plate. Spoon the tomato mixture over the rosti with the crème fraîche (if using) and serve straight away.

Teriyaki Cauliflower and Sticky Rice Bowls

This is a simple recipe of many moving parts, so let me run you through a few shortcuts and considerations. They'll allow you to gauge how much labour you're prepared to exert ...

I've stipulated nutty, brown sushi rice here, which is fabulous in all ways but time-consuming to soak and cook; you can obviously use a white version or any other grain you prefer, ready-cooked or not.

Don't even think about chopping fresh turmeric without gloves on, especially if you wear pale gel nail polish. You have been warned. But you'll thank me for the golden, turmeric eggs, which are a thing of beauty.

Make the teriyaki sauce and the pickled beets a day or several days ahead of time. It's perfectly acceptable to cheat with raw or softer, ready-pickled beetroot, but I'd make your own teriyaki, if possible. It will have bags more character and less sugar than a bought one.

Other things you could add to the bowls include: avocado, snipped strips of toasted nori seaweed, roasted cubes of pumpkin, turmeric-fried tofu for vegans (avoid honey elsewhere in the recipe). And, of course, you can double this to serve four or give yourself leftovers, but I promise it's worth the trouble for two.

SERVES 2 .... GENEROUSLY
PREPARATION TIME .... 1 HOUR 15 MINUTES
COOKING TIME .... 50 MINUTES

FOR THE PICKLED BEETROOT (BEETS)

150g (5oz) beetroot (1 large), peeled and cut into
    fine matchsticks
1 tbsp maple syrup or mild honey
2 tbsp rice wine vinegar
1 pinch of salt

FOR THE TERIYAKI SAUCE

3 tbsp maple syrup or mild honey
4 tbsp tamari or light soy sauce
2 tbsp finely grated fresh ginger root
2 garlic cloves, crushed

FOR THE REST

190g (6½oz) brown sushi rice
1 medium cauliflower, trimmed and cut into
    8 wedges through the core
3½ tbsp groundnut (peanut) oil
8 slender spring onions (scallions), trimmed
20g (¾oz) fresh turmeric, peeled and sliced into
    very fine matchsticks
2 large, very fresh eggs
2 heaped tsp shichimi togarashi seasoning
salt and freshly ground black pepper

Simply toss the beetroot matchsticks with the honey, rice vinegar and a pinch of salt. Cover and chill for at least an hour before eating; the longer they are left, the more pickled they will become.

To make the teriyaki sauce – which can also be finished a few days ahead of time and kept chilled – put all the ingredients in a saucepan with 175ml (6fl oz) water and dissolve over a low heat, stirring. Bring to the boil and simmer gently for 5 minutes. Let cool.

On the day or evening you want to eat, start by placing the brown sushi rice in a medium saucepan with 600ml (20fl oz) of cool water and a pinch of salt. Set aside for 40 minutes or so.

Preheat the oven to 200°C (400°F/gas 6).

Set the rice pan over a lowish heat and bring slowly to the boil, then partially cover with a lid and simmer for about 30–35 minutes until the rice is just tender, not soggy, and the water has been absorbed. Use straight away or cover with a clean tea (dish) towel and the lid, setting aside for up to 30 minutes until needed. It will stay warm enough and not suffer greatly.

Meanwhile, coat the cauliflower wedges with 1½ tablespoons of the oil and season well with black pepper. Roast in a roasting pan for 25 minutes, then turn the wedges over and coat them with a quarter of the teriyaki sauce, drizzling or brushing it on. Return the tray to the oven for 12–15 minutes more until the wedges are caramelized and tender.

Coat the trimmed spring onions with ½ tablespoon of the oil and put a griddle

pan over a very high heat until smoking hot. Chargrill the onions for 4 minutes in total, turning halfway, until slightly charred.

To make the eggs, put the turmeric matchsticks in a non-stick frying pan (skillet) with the remaining 1½ tablespoons of groundnut oil and a pinch of salt. Set the cold pan over a lowish heat and after 2–3 minutes, once the turmeric is gently fizzing and sizzling, break in the eggs, spacing them well apart and flipping the sizzling turmeric up onto the whites. Fry the eggs slowly, for about 4 minutes, flicking the whites with the golden oil until they are lacy-edged, with set whites and still-wobbling yolks. Remove the pan from the heat and season the eggs.

Divide the cooked rice between warmed bowls and top with a couple of cauliflower wedges. Tuck the drained, pickled beets alongside with the charred spring onions, carefully balancing a golden egg on top of each bowl. Spoon a generous amount of teriyaki sauce over (you'll likely have leftovers) and scatter with shichimi togarashi seasoning to finish.

NOTE

The pickled beets can be made a few days ahead of time and kept chilled.

Winter

Mushroom and Chard Quesadillas with Red Chimichurri

By far the easiest way to make the red chimichurri (essential, by the way, adding smoky, verdant, garlicky flavour – without it, these inauthentic quesadillas will be lacking) is using a mini food processor, or the small bowl of a large one. Alternatively, you can use a large knife and some patience to chop the chillies, garlic and herbs, then combine with the oil and vinegar in a bowl to make a rustic paste. A pestle and mortar will work, too.

SERVES 2 .... AS A MAIN OR 4 AS A SNACK
PREPARATION TIME .... 25 MINUTES
COOKING TIME .... 50 MINUTES

FOR THE RED CHIMICHURRI

2 red chillies, left whole
2 garlic cloves, chopped
5 tbsp extra virgin olive oil
½ tsp smoked paprika
2 tbsp red wine vinegar
½ small bunch of flat-leaf parsley with
    stalks, chopped
½ small bunch of coriander (cilantro) with
    stalks, chopped
½ tsp dried oregano
salt and freshly ground black pepper

FOR THE QUESADILLAS

2 tbsp mild olive oil or groundnut (peanut) oil
3 garlic cloves, finely chopped
200g (7oz) bunch of rainbow or Swiss chard, stalks
    chopped and leaves shredded
3 field mushrooms, thinly sliced
150g (5oz) oyster mushrooms, shredded
180g (6½oz) king oyster mushrooms, thinly sliced
75g (3oz) mature Cheddar, coarsely grated
1 mozzarella ball, drained and finely diced
8 x 15cm (6in) diameter corn tortillas

TO SERVE

sliced avocado
lime wedges
coriander (cilantro) leaves
Pickleback Ruby Slaw (see page 192)

Start with the chimichurri. Use tongs to hold the chillies over a low gas flame, turning for 3–4 minutes until blistered and charred all over. If you don't have gas or a barbecue option, a grill set to high or even a smoking-hot frying pan (skillet) will do a similar job of charring the chillies. Then, lop off the stalks and add to the food processor with everything but the fresh herbs. Blitz to a rough paste, scraping down the sides as needed. Add the herbs with 2 tablespoons of water and blitz again until the chimichurri resembles a rustic pesto. Adjust the seasoning and even the vinegar/paprika to taste; it should be punchy and vibrant. Set aside.

Put the 2 tablespoons oil for the filling in a large frying pan set over a low-medium heat. Add the garlic, chard stalks and mushrooms and cook, stirring often until reduced in volume and golden. This is a slow process and will take about 25 minutes.

Add the shredded chard leaves with 1 tablespoon of the chimichurri. Stir-fry for 2–3 minutes, pressing down on the beans with a wooden spoon, to crush and heat through while wilting the greens. Remove from the heat and season to taste.

Turn the oven to low to keep the cooked quesadillas warm. Combine the cheeses in a bowl and place a flat griddle or large frying pan over a medium heat. After a minute or so, add one tortilla to the dry pan, sprinkle a little cheese (about an eighth, if you're counting) over then top along with a quarter of the mushroom mixture. Top with a little more cheese and a second tortilla, pressing down firmly.

Cook for a couple of minutes until lightly browned, then carefully flip and cook for a further 2 minutes until pale golden with a melty filling. Keep warm in a low oven while repeating to make 4 quesadillas. Slice into

quarters and serve with the red chimichurri
to spoon over, ripe avocado, lime wedges
to squeeze, extra coriander and perhaps the
Pickleback Slaw from page 192 in this chapter.

NOTE

Stretch the deeply savoury, mushroom quesadilla
filling further by adding a tin of drained black beans
with the chard leaves, crushing them down in the
pan with the back of a spoon.

Pickleback Ruby Slaw

A magnificent, shredded slaw to celebrate inky purples and reds. It isn't from anywhere in particular but has a hint of Texas barbecue about the pickle dressing and the pecans and will add inauthentic contrast to tacos or quesadillas, such as the mushroom and chard ones in this chapter (page 190).

You can play around with this by adding chilli (hot pepper) flakes, caraway seeds, celery seeds, coriander seeds, etc. – pretty much any spice that might be used in a pickle – to make the most of the pickle juice used in the dressing.

VEGAN

SERVES 4–6 .... AS A SIDE
PREPARATION TIME .... 30 MINUTES

FOR THE DRESSING

1 small echalion or banana shallot, halved and very
    finely chopped
3 tbsp pickle juice (from a gherkin or cornichon jar)
1 tbsp maple syrup
1 tsp fennel seeds
1 heaped tsp wholegrain mustard
4 tbsp mild olive oil
1 small bunch of dill, finely chopped
salt and freshly ground black pepper

FOR THE SLAW

60g (2oz) pecans, chopped
10 cornichons, drained and finely chopped
350g (12oz/1 small) cored red cabbage, halved and
    very finely sliced
1 small cauliflower, trimmed and finely sliced,
    including any tender leaves
2 beetroot (beets), candy if possible, peeled and
    finely sliced
200g (7oz) radishes, finely sliced
2 small red apples, halved, cored and finely sliced
1 echalion or banana shallot, finely sliced
    into rounds
2 red chicory (endive) heads, trimmed and shredded
1 punnet of purple radish sprouts, snipped
salt and freshly ground black pepper

To make the dressing, put all the ingredients in a lidded jar with 2 tablespoons of warm water and a little salt and pepper. Shake vigorously to emulsify.

Put all the slaw ingredients in a large bowl and toss the dressing through. Check for seasoning and serve on a platter.

Winter

NOTE

If you can't find purple radish sprouts, substitute with snipped mustard cress or even basil leaves.

Celeriac, Date and Preserved Lemon Salad

A low-effort salad with big flavours, rather unusually based on raw celeriac (celery root) (unusual, given that it isn't a remoulade). Cutting the vegetable finely is key here; if you don't have the patience for chopping but are brave enough to use a mandoline, shave the celeriac into paper-fine slices instead of matchsticks. I love to use cinnamon judiciously in savoury recipes and it works especially well with this profile of dates, preserved lemon rind and deeply toasty almonds.

VEGAN
SERVES 4 _____ AS A SIDE
PREPARATION TIME _____ 20 MINUTES
COOKING TIME _____ 8 MINUTES

6 tbsp extra virgin olive oil
1kg (2lb 4oz) celeriac (celery root)
juice of 2 lemons
1 handful of ice cubes
1 red onion, halved and very finely sliced
1 red chilli, finely sliced
1 small bunch of flat-leaf parsley, stalks and
    leaves chopped
100g (3½oz) blanched or flaked (slivered) almonds
zest of 2 preserved lemons, very finely sliced
½ tsp ground cinnamon
100g (3½oz) stoned Medjool dates, sliced
    into slivers
salt and freshly ground black pepper

Pare the outer layer of skin and all the knobbly bits from the celeriac to leave a smooth orb. Slice this into fine rounds and then into matchsticks. Cutting the unwieldy celeriac into halves or quarters first can make this process easier. Submerge the matchsticks in a large bowlful of cool water with half of the lemon juice and a handful of ice cubes. Set aside for 15 minutes.

Meanwhile, put 2 tablespoons of the oil in a large frying pan (skillet) set over a low-medium heat. Add the red onion, chilli and chopped parsley stalks. If using blanched almonds, add them here; if slivered, add halfway through. Cook for 7–8 minutes in total, stirring until the onion begins to frazzle at the edges and the nuts turn gold. Add the preserved lemon peel and cinnamon. Stir through for about a minute, then remove from heat.

Drain the celeriac well, patting the slices dry with a tea (dish) towel. Tip into a bowl with the fried onion mixture, parsley leaves, dates, remaining lemon juice and the remaining 4 tablespoons of olive oil. Toss through, adjust the seasoning to taste and mix again.

Winter

Warm Salad of Griddled Radicchio and Borlotti

This is a quietly sophisticated, winter salad plate. Frying the drained borlotti beans until their jackets burst open and turn crisp, revealing fluffy insides, is a simple and excellent trick to borrow for other salads, risottos and pasta. Spoon the beans over sweet, bitter, charred chicory (endives), with the jolt of a mint-heavy Salsa Verde (see page 219), and you've got a winner.

VEGAN
SERVES 4
PREPARATION TIME _____ 20 MINUTES
COOKING TIME _____ 10 MINUTES

1 quantity of Salsa Verde (see page 219)
2 tbsp olive oil
2 x 400g (14oz) tins of borlotti beans, drained, rinsed and patted dry
1 tbsp red wine vinegar
3 red radicchio, halved or quartered depending on size
4 red chicory (Belgian endive) bulbs, halved
1 tbsp chopped chives

TO SERVE

extra virgin olive oil
toasted sourdough slices (optional)

Start by making the salsa verde as described on page 219.

To make the salad, put 1 tablespoon of the olive oil in a large frying pan (skillet) set over a high heat. Add the dry beans and stir-fry for 90 seconds or so until their jackets are crisp and bursting open, revealing their fluffy interiors. Add the vinegar, bubble down to nothing and set aside.

Drizzle the radicchio and chicory with oil. Get a griddle pan smoking-hot, then add them to the pan and cook until well marked with grill lines. Arrange on serving plates with the crisp borlotti beans, salsa verde, chives, a good drizzle of extra virgin olive oil and slices of toasted sourdough, if liked.

Baked Wedges
with Mushrooms and Tomatoes

These tomato-cloaked, baked wedges with mushrooms look unassuming from a glance at the ingredients list, but please don't let that put you off making them. The recipe is far more special than you'd think, inspired by beautiful Greek and Cypriot ways with tomato-y roast potatoes. Admittedly, the variety of potato you choose to use matters here and an old, floury number won't bring the same magic. The best to choose are the buttermilk-yellow, waxen, Cypriot spuds I use in the potato gratin on page 212.

To make this into an easy brunch, crack very fresh eggs directly into the dish at the end of cooking, returning it to the oven for a few minutes to set them, and serve with buttered spinach.

VEGAN

SERVES 4	AS A SIDE
PREPARATION TIME	25 MINUTES
COOKING TIME	55 MINUTES

30g (1oz) dried porcini
1.2kg (2lb 6oz) waxy Cypriot potatoes, cut into
    long wedges
6 tbsp extra virgin olive oil
6 oregano sprigs, leaves stripped
300g (10½oz) king oyster mushrooms, sliced
6 fat garlic cloves, sliced
1 heaped tbsp tomato purée (paste)
400g (14oz) tin of finely chopped tomatoes
salt and freshly ground black pepper

Preheat the oven to 200°C (400°F/gas 6).

Cover the dried porcini with 200ml (7fl oz) of just-boiled water in a bowl and set aside for 20 minutes or so.

Combine the potatoes, oil, oregano and sliced mushrooms in a very large baking dish or tin (at least 30 x 40cm/12 x 16in, big enough to hold them in a single layer) and season well.

Roast for 20 minutes, then add the garlic, stirring through to coat with oil and return to the oven for 5 minutes.

Combine the soaked porcini and porcini water, tomato purée and tinned tomatoes and pour this mixture into the dish, shuffling to coat the wedges without breaking them up. Slide the dish into the oven for 30 minutes, carefully stirring through halfway, until the sauce coating the potatoes is rich and thick. Serve as a characterful side, or scatter with the feta, parsley and lemon salad described in the note.

Winter

NOTE

This dish works as a side, but I like to serve it as a main, topped with a simple salad of crumbled feta, black olives, thinly sliced red onion, parsley leaves and chopped lemon flesh.

Parsnip, Kale and Pecorino
Spelt Risotto with Walnuts

An easy and wholesome supper for cold days and hungry people. The grated parsnip is incorporated into the 'risotto', along with shredded kale, to imbue it with sweetness as it bakes. Finish each bowlful with wedges of baked parsnip, pecorino and a shower of toasted, chopped walnuts.

Do check that the pecorino you buy is vegetarian (some are made with animal rennet) and sub in a vegetarian parmesan-style cheese or a hard goat's cheese if not.

SERVES 3–4 _____ **AS A MAIN**
PREPARATION TIME _____ **20 MINUTES**
COOKING TIME _____ **55 MINUTES**

700g (1lb 9oz) slender, medium-sized parsnips, ends trimmed
30g (1oz) unsalted butter
2½ tbsp olive oil
1 sweet onion, halved and finely chopped
850ml (30fl oz) vegetable stock
300g (10½oz) pearled spelt
150ml (5fl oz) dry white wine
1 handful of thyme sprigs
2 tsp honey
50g (1¾oz) walnut halves, roughly crushed
finely grated zest and juice of 1 lemon
300g (10½oz) cavolo nero or other kale, stalks removed, leaves thickly sliced
100g (3½oz) hard pecorino, finely grated
salt and freshly ground black pepper

Preheat the oven to 200°C (400°F/gas 6) and make sure there's room to fit a casserole in the middle.

If the parsnips have smooth and unblemished skin, just give them a scrub, otherwise, peel them. Coarsely grate 400g (14oz) of the chunkier parsnips, cutting the remainder into slender quarters or sixths, lengthways, according to size.

Put a medium flameproof casserole or similar ovenproof saucepan with a lid onto a low heat and melt half of the butter with 1 tablespoon of the oil. Add the onion with a large pinch of salt and cook gently, stirring often, for about 10 minutes until translucent and colouring slightly.

Bring the stock up to simmering point in a separate saucepan and keep at the barest bubble.

Turn up the heat under the onion pan to medium and tip in the grated parsnips and spelt, stirring to coat in the fat for a minute. Add the wine and cook off until no liquid remains, then add all of the hot stock to the casserole. Cover with the lid and slide into the oven for 40 minutes.

Meanwhile, spread the prepared, slender parsnips out in a roasting pan. Toss with the remaining 1½ tablespoons of oil, season well with salt and pepper and dot with the remaining butter. Roast for 15–20 minutes, shimmying the tin halfway through, until turning golden. Now add most of the thyme sprigs with the honey and walnuts. Return to the oven for a further 10 minutes until everything is toasted and the parsnips are tender. Remove from the oven and add the lemon zest with half of the lemon juice.

Stir the shredded cavolo nero into the spelt and return to the oven for 5 minutes. Remove from the oven, stir in half of the pecorino with the remaining lemon juice and leave to sit for a couple of minutes. Check the seasoning and serve in warmed bowls with the remaining pecorino and the roast parsnip mixture on top, garnished with a couple of thyme sprigs.

Beetroot and Caper Burgers

A hearty vegetarian burger – based on beetroot (beets) and lentils with hits
of salty, fried capers – to serve with potato wedges, perhaps baked with rosemary
and olive oil, and a leafy salad. Pub food to cook at home.

SERVES 4
PREPARATION TIME 20 MINUTES
COOKING TIME 1 HOUR 40 MINUTES

2 tbsp mayonnaise
2 tbsp Greek yoghurt
2½ tbsp olive oil
4 tbsp capers, rinsed and drained
400g (14oz) tin of green lentils, well-drained
1 egg
1 handful of flat-leaf parsley leaves
1 tsp fennel or celery seeds
100g (3½oz) soft breadcrumbs
75g (2½oz) sunflower seeds
1 red onion, finely chopped
400g (14oz) beetroot (beets) (3 large), peeled and
    coarsely grated
4 brioche buns, split horizontally
1 handful of wild rocket (arugula)
100g (3½oz) ready-pickled beetroot, sliced
1 ripe avocado, halved, stoned and sliced
salt and freshly ground black pepper

Preheat the oven to 190°C (375°F/gas 5).

Combine the mayonnaise and yoghurt in a small bowl, season and set aside in the fridge.

Put 1 tablespoon of the oil in a frying pan (skillet) set over a medium heat and add half of the capers. Fry for 1–2 minutes until opened-up, golden and crisp. Tip out onto paper towel to drain and set aside.

Put the lentils and egg in the small bowl of a food processor and blitz to a nubbly purée. Now add the parsley, fennel or celery seeds and the remaining capers. Blitz again to chop quite finely. Transfer to a large mixing bowl and stir in the breadcrumbs and sunflower seeds.

Soften the red onion and a pinch of salt in 1 tablespoon of the oil in a frying pan set over a medium heat. Stir often for about 7 minutes until the onion is soft and beginning to brown. Add the grated beetroot and stir-fry for 10 minutes until soft and 'dry'. Let cool, then tip into the mixing bowl with the lentil mixture and fold together. Season.

Line a large baking (cookie) sheet with baking parchment. Form the mixture into four, burger-shaped patties with wet hands and space out on the parchment. Brush the tops and sides with the remaining oil and bake for 25 minutes until firm and beginning to brown.

Either warm the split brioche buns through in the oven for the last 3 minutes of cooking time or char-grill their cut sides in a smoking-hot griddle pan for around 30 seconds until well marked with lines.

Spread the base half of each warmed bun with the mayo mixture and the fried capers. Layer some rocket leaves on top of that, top with a beetroot burger and finish each with pickled beet slices, avocado, more rocket and the bun tops.

Potato and Rice Pilaf
with Saffron and Cherries

A gentle but magnificent spiced pilaf and one of my favourite recipes in the book, special enough to be the centrepiece of a celebratory supper, perhaps with baked, spiced aubergine (eggplant). This is heavily inspired by the stunning pilafs of Persia, but with potatoes at the forefront, the fluffy, buttery rice bolstered by plenty of dill, dried cherries and pomegranate.

SERVES 4–6
PREPARATION TIME .... **20 MINUTES**
COOKING TIME .... **1 HOUR 10 MINUTES**

250g (9oz) basmati rice, rinsed and drained
400g (14oz) tin of green lentils, rinsed and drained
1 pinch of saffron strands
60g (2oz) salted butter
1 large onion, chopped
6 green cardamom pods, bruised
1½ tsp cumin seeds, crushed
1½ tsp coriander seeds, crushed
½ tsp ground cinnamon or ½ cinnamon stick
30g (1oz) fresh ginger root, peeled and
    finely chopped
4 wide strips of pared lemon zest
600g (1lb 5oz) large, waxy, baking-size potatoes,
    scrubbed and diced into 2cm (¾in) pieces
2 garlic cloves, finely chopped
100g (3½oz) dried cherries
1 large bunch of dill, finely chopped
100g (3½oz) full-fat Greek yoghurt
1 small pomegranate, arils only
salt and freshly ground black pepper

NOTE
You could swap the potatoes out for celeriac (celery root) or parsnip, if preferred, or use a combination of all three.

Put the rinsed rice in a large saucepan with 300ml (10fl oz) water and a pinch of salt. Bring to the boil, then turn the heat down to a gentle simmer and cover with a lid. Leave to cook for 8 minutes until the water has been absorbed, then remove from the heat. Add the tinned lentils and fluff through the rice with a fork.

Preheat the oven to 190°C (375°F/gas 5).

Put the saffron in a small bowl and cover with 90ml (3fl oz) boiling water. Set aside for 10 minutes.

Melt half of the butter and the oil in a medium flameproof casserole. Add the onion with a pinch of salt and cook over a lowish heat for 10 minutes, stirring often, until soft and golden. Stir in all the spices, the ginger and lemon zest, stirring for 1–2 minutes, followed by the potatoes. Turn up the heat a touch and stir-fry for about 5 minutes. Add the garlic and cook for 7 minutes or so until the potatoes begin to caramelize. If the mixture is catching at any point, turn the heat down slightly and/or add a touch more butter or oil. The potatoes won't be cooked through but should be partially soft and golden on the outside. Tip everything into a bowl and stir in the dried cherries, two-thirds of the chopped dill, a generous season of black pepper and a little salt.

Stir 2 generously heaped tablespoons of the rice and lentil mixture into the yoghurt in a small bowl. Melt the remaining butter in the unrinsed casserole set over a low heat. Drop teaspoonfuls of the yoghurt rice all over the base of the pan to cover it evenly. Top with another couple of heaped tablespoons of rice and lentils, filling in any gaps. Now spoon the potato-dill mixture over in an even layer and top with the remaining rice and lentils. Spoon the steeped-saffron water across the surface and cover tightly with the lid. Bake in the middle of the oven for 30 minutes. Let the casserole rest for 5 minutes, then scatter with the pomegranate arils and the remaining dill.

Winter

Roast Cauliflower with Crisp Breadcrumbs

A more luxurious recipe than the title implies, this whole, roast cauliflower is cloaked in a Moorish-inspired affair of smoky, saffron dressing and sweet-salty-sour-crisp crumbs. Toasted breadcrumbs are the penny-pinching choice; golden pine nuts, almonds or walnuts would all make luxurious additions or even substitutes.

SERVES 4–6 — WITH SIDES
PREPARATION TIME — 25 MINUTES
COOKING TIME — 1 HOUR 35 MINUTES

2 tsp sweet smoked paprika
4 garlic cloves, crushed
5 tbsp extra virgin olive oil, to taste
1 extra-large (1.5kg/3lb 5oz) cauliflower, tough or
    excess outer leaves removed and base trimmed
1 large pinch of saffron strands, steeped in
    2 tbsp just-boiled water
1½ tbsp honey
3 tbsp sherry vinegar
2 tsp finely chopped rosemary leaves (or thyme)
90g (3oz) sourdough breadcrumbs
2 tbsp capers, rinsed and drained
finely grated zest and juice of 1 small lemon
50g (1¾oz) flame raisins
1 small bunch of flat-leaf parsley, chopped
salt and freshly ground black pepper

TO SERVE

chicory (endive) or rocket (arugula) salad
mustard-dressed lentils

Preheat the oven to 190°C (375°F/gas 5).

Combine the paprika and 2 of the crushed garlic cloves with 2 tablespoons of the olive oil. Season well with salt and pepper and rub the mixture over the surface of the cauliflower. Set it in a large casserole, cover with the lid and roast in the middle of the oven for about 1 hour 20 minutes, or until tender when a skewer is poked in.

Meanwhile, combine the steeped saffron, honey, sherry vinegar, rosemary and 1 tablespoon of the olive oil in a small bowl. Season well and set aside.

Put the final 2 tablespoons of olive oil in a large frying pan (skillet) set over a medium heat. Add the 2 remaining crushed garlic cloves and stir for a few seconds. Tip in the breadcrumbs, capers, lemon zest and raisins, stirring around for 4–5 minutes until golden and crisp (the oil will be absorbed – feel free to add a little more if you like). Remove from the heat and season. When cool, stir in the chopped parsley.

Now remove the lid from the cauliflower, spoon the saffron dressing over and continue to roast for 10 minutes until golden. Either keep the cauliflower in the pot and take straight to the table or carefully transfer to a serving platter and squeeze the lemon juice over the top. Spoon the crisp breadcrumbs over the top to serve, letting some fall down into the cooking juices at the sides. A chicory or rocket salad and perhaps some mustard-dressed lentils go well here too.

Beetroot, Lentil and Coconut Soup

Beetroot (beets) always bring the drama and can stand up to robust spices and aromatics, but you could certainly swap in roast cubes of butternut squash or parsnip for those who don't appreciate its earthy sweetness. You can make the soup base up to three days ahead of time and reheat thoroughly, but don't stint on the frazzled ginger and curry leaf topping, made to order so it's still sizzling from the pan.

VEGAN
SERVES 4
PREPARATION TIME _____ 20 MINUTES
COOKING TIME _____ 1 HOUR

2 tbsp coconut oil or groundnut (peanut) oil
1 large red onion, chopped
3 large thumbs of fresh ginger root, peeled
1 tsp fennel seeds
5 green cardamom pods, seeds only
1 large pinch of dried chilli (hot pepper) flakes
150g (5oz) red lentils, rinsed
500g (1lb 2oz) red beetroot (beets), peeled and
    roughly chopped
800ml (28fl oz) vegetable stock
400ml (14fl oz) tin of thick coconut milk,
    well-shaken
2 tsp garam masala
1 red chilli, sliced
about 20 fresh curry leaves
juice of 1 large lemon
salt and freshly ground black pepper

Put 1 tablespoon of the oil in a large saucepan set over a low heat. Add the onion with a pinch of salt and cook, stirring, for 10 minutes until translucent. Roughly chop 2 of the ginger thumbs and add to the pan. Turn the heat up a notch and continue to cook for 5 minutes.

Stir in the fennel seeds, cardamom seeds, chilli flakes and red lentils, giving the spices a minute to warm through and toast. Add the beetroot, stock and 250ml (8½fl oz) of the coconut milk, stir well, turn up the heat and bring to the boil. Now reduce the heat to a gentle simmer and cook for 25–30 minutes until the beetroot and lentils are completely tender, stirring now and then to prevent the lentils sticking to the base of the pan. Stir in the garam masala and simmer for a further 5 minutes. Blend the soup in batches until velvet-smooth (take your time to really blend it here, preferably using an upright blender for best results). Return to the pan, gently heat through and keep warm.

Slice the remaining thumb of ginger into fine matchsticks. Put the remaining tablespoon of oil in a frying pan (skillet) set over a medium heat and add the ginger and sliced chilli. Season with salt and pepper and sizzle, stirring for 1–2 minutes until the ginger begins to frazzle. Throw in the curry leaves and stir to coat in the oil. After a few seconds they will begin to darken and look shiny. Remove the pan from the heat.

Stir the lemon juice into the hot soup and adjust the seasoning as needed. Divide between warmed bowls and finish with a swirl of the remaining coconut milk and the sizzled ginger mixture.

Winter

Gratin of Greens, Potatoes and Mushrooms

Good ingredients are essential for time-consuming but seemingly simple recipes like this. I don't mean expensive, per se, just well sourced and that means going to a certain amount of trouble when it comes to potatoes. Yellow waxen Cypriot spuds, sold in my local Turkish shop, still cloaked in mud; mature spinach with flag-like leaves and toothsome stalks to chop; buttermilk-coloured crème fraîche, with a voluptuous texture from high fat content. If you don't have those things, you can make it anyway, of course you can ... but it'll just be a standard gratin without the quiet magic properly good ingredients bring. Note the essential 15–20-minute rest at the end of the cooking time.

SERVES 4

PREPARATION TIME	30 MINUTES
COOKING TIME	2 HOURS 20 MINUTES
RESTING TIME	20 MINUTES

50g (1¾oz) salted butter, softened, plus extra for the dish
1.3kg (2lb 8oz) yellow waxy potatoes (Cypriot), peeled
15g (½oz) dried porcini mushrooms, crumbled into small pieces
2 sweet white onions, halved and sliced
300g (10½oz) mushrooms, sliced – can be button or fancier/porcini, etc.
500g (1lb 2oz) greens, such as chard, baby greens or large-leaf spinach or kale
1 tbsp finely chopped sage, plus 12 whole sage leaves
300ml (10fl oz) vegetable stock
50ml (1¾fl oz) dry white wine
300g (10½oz) full-fat and best-quality crème fraîche
salt and freshly ground black pepper

Lightly butter a 25cm (10in) square ovenproof dish.

Slice the potatoes lengthways, preferably using a mandoline, or just patience and a very sharp knife. They should be about 3mm (⅛in) thick; not so thin that they break up, but not so thick that they aren't slightly pliable.

Gently simmer the sliced potatoes in plenty of boiling water for 5–6 minutes only. Very carefully pour the potatoes and their water into a large colander in the sink. The aim is to keep the slices perfectly intact.

Meanwhile, steep the dried porcini mushrooms in 3 tablespoons of boiling water in a bowl. Set aside for 10 minutes, then squeeze the mushrooms out over the bowl and keep both components on hand.

Put the 50g (1¾oz) butter in a large flameproof casserole or saucepan and add the onions with a pinch of salt. Cook over a lowish heat, stirring, for 20 minutes until the onion is very soft but not coloured. Add the fresh mushrooms and cook for 5 minutes, followed by the greens, the squeezed-out porcini mushrooms and the chopped sage, stir-frying for about 4 minutes until the greens have wilted. Season generously with salt and pepper.

Preheat the oven to 180°C (350°F/gas 4).

Put the vegetable stock, white wine, porcini water and crème fraîche in a saucepan and simmer down for 10 minutes until the volume has reduced by about a third.

Overlap half of the potatoes in the base of the dish to cover it evenly, seasoning as you go. Pile the greens and onion mixture on top and pour over a third of the crème fraîche mixture. Top with the rest of the potatoes, again seasoning as you go and layering them neatly, tucking the whole sage leaves in to finish. Carefully pour the rest of the crème fraîche mixture over – it will be brimming to the top

Winter

of the dish, so go slowly, stopping to jiggle the dish and allow the sauce to find its level.

Cover with kitchen foil and cook for 35 minutes. Then turn the oven down to 170°C (340°F/gas 3), remove the foil and cook for a further hour until the gratin is golden and completely tender to the point of a knife. Rest for 15–20 minutes before slicing and serving – this step will allow the gratin to settle and slice perfectly, so factor it into your cooking timings.

NOTE

Resting a potato gratin, or indeed a lasagne, for a few minutes after cooking gives everything time to settle as it cools, making for neater slices.

Winter

Beetroot Risotto with Crisp Sage and Crème Fraîche

A supper party classic to emphasize that simple, vegetarian food can be sophisticated and understated. Be delicate when cooking the rice, stirring in one direction as the Italians do and aiming for the just-tender rice to 'flow' across the plate, rather than sitting in a sticky clag.

SERVES 4
PREPARATION TIME _____ **20 MINUTES**
COOKING TIME _____ **25 MINUTES**

1.1 litres (37fl oz) vegetable stock
25g (1oz) unsalted butter
2 tbsp olive oil
1 small red onion, finely chopped
150ml (5fl oz) red wine
275g (10oz) Arborio or other risotto rice
2 medium beetroot (beets), peeled and
    coarsely grated
50g (1¾oz) vegetarian parmesan-style cheese,
    finely grated
1 handful of sage leaves
4 tbsp best crème fraîche
salt and freshly ground black pepper

Put the stock in a medium saucepan and bring to the boil. Cover the stock pan with a lid and return to a low heat to simmer gently.

Melt the butter and 1 tablespoon of the oil in a deep-sided frying pan (skillet) and add the onion. Cook over a low heat for 10 minutes, stirring often until soft but not coloured.

Increase the heat slightly and add the rice, stirring to coat it in the butter for about a minute. Pour the wine into the pan, allowing it to evaporate away to almost nothing. Stir in the grated beets and 1 ladleful of the simmering stock. Simmer, stirring until the stock has all but disappeared before adding a second ladleful. Keep stirring, simmering and adding stock in this way for about 18 minutes until the rice is tender, but retains a bit of bite. The mixture should be loose and flowing in texture. Remove from the heat, stir in half of the vegetarian parmesan and season to taste with salt and pepper.

Meanwhile, in a frying pan set over a medium heat, gently fry the sage leaves in the remaining olive oil for a minute or two until fizzing but not coloured (they will crisp upon cooling). Season with salt and pepper and drain on paper towel.

Divide the risotto between shallow bowls and dot scant teaspoonfuls of crème fraîche over, scattering with the sage leaves and remaining vegetarian parmesan to finish.

SAUCES

This section contains a few basic, useful and
notable sauces used in the book to enhance
and showcase vegetables, including some
interesting variations.

Vegan Thai Red Curry Paste

No funky Thai shrimp paste included here, for obvious reasons, but this recipe still makes a highly flavoured, extremely hot (be warned) and authentic-tasting paste to use as a base for vegetable and coconut milk curries, or to make the dreamy, cashew satay sauce featured in the Spicy Tofu-Cashew Satay Bowls with Grilled Asparagus and Edamame (see page 110).

MAKES ABOUT 6 TBSP
SERVES 2 X 4-PERSON CURRIES
PREPARATION TIME 30 MINUTES

6 dried long red chillies
1½ tsp cumin seeds
1 tsp coriander seeds
8 white peppercorns
½ tsp ground cinnamon
2 tsp sweet smoked paprika
1 scant tsp salt
4 red bird's eye chillies, chopped
3 fresh coriander roots or ½ small bunch
   of coriander (cilantro) stalks
1 large thumb of galangal or fresh ginger root,
   peeled and chopped
3 Thai or red shallots
2 lemongrass stalks, trimmed and roughly chopped
3 fresh lime leaves, roughly chopped
10 garlic cloves
a little water and/or groundnut (peanut) oil,
   as needed

Ideally, wear gloves to make this recipe in case you get distracted and rub your eye or worse, as the chilli oil will make them sting.

Put the dried chillies in a heatproof bowl and cover with just-boiled water. Set aside for 10 minutes, then drain and roughly chop.

Put the cumin and coriander seeds and the white peppercorns in a dry frying pan (skillet) set over a medium heat. Toast for a minute or so, shaking the pan, until fragrant. Add the cinnamon and paprika and toast for 30 seconds more, then roughly grind the spices in a pestle and mortar or using the base of a sturdy jam jar.

If using a pestle and mortar, add the soaked chillies to it with the fresh bird's eye chillies and salt and begin to pound to a paste. Otherwise, tip the spices and chillies into a mini food processor. Pound or blitz to crush or chop, stopping to add the coriander roots or stalks and the galangal or ginger. Pound or blitz again, stopping to scrape down the sides in the latter case. Now add the shallots, lemongrass, lime leaves and garlic, continuing to pound or blitz to a relatively uniform paste. It doesn't have to be too smooth, but you will probably need to add a little water and/or groundnut oil to get the blades moving in the food processor.

That's it – a curry paste to make your eyes water. Keep it covered in the fridge for a week or so, or wrap well and freeze for as long as several weeks (any longer and it will be perfectly safe to eat, but will begin to lose its vigour). To use and make the best of it, fry the paste slowly in a generous amount of oil to gently caramelize the ingredients. Cook low for around 10 minutes, before continuing with the recipe.

Sauces

Summer Herb Pesto

Make this with all basil, as is traditional, or swap half the quantity below for any combination of Greek basil, mint, flat-leaf parsley, chervil or green carrot tops.

MAKES ABOUT 200G (7OZ/HALF A MEDIUM JAR)
PREPARATION TIME .... **15 MINUTES**

2 garlic cloves, roughly chopped
1 large pinch of sea salt flakes
1 large bunch of basil
50g (1¾oz) pine nuts or blanched almonds,
  lightly toasted
about 100ml (3½fl oz) extra virgin olive oil,
  plus extra to cover
25g (1oz) vegetarian parmesan-style cheese,
  finely grated

Either pound this pesto together in a pestle and mortar in traditional style, starting with the garlic cloves and a pinch of sea salt, first making a paste then gradually adding the basil, pine nuts or almonds, pounding together as you add the olive oil in a steady stream, being mindful not to turn the herb leaves to sludge and only stirring in the cheese at the end.

To make it in a small processor, start with the garlic and a good pinch of sea salt. Blitz to chop, then add the basil and blitz again. Scrape down the sides and throw in the pine nuts or almonds with a good glug of olive oil. Pulse, dribbling olive oil into the processor with the blades still moving to make a bright green, textured paste. Stir in the cheese.

To store, spoon the pesto into a jar, level the top and cover with a thin layer of olive oil, followed by the jar lid. It will keep in the fridge for a week or so.

Kale and Toasted Nut Pesto

An excellent, forgiving pesto to dress up any number of pastas, salads and soups. This is the one to use, with hazelnuts for preference, in the Summer Lasagne (see page 80). For other recipes, try adding a chopped red chilli for a touch of heat or using unblanched watercress (or rocket/arugula or any sort of kale) in place of the cavolo nero.

MAKES ABOUT 200G (7OZ/HALF A MEDIUM JAR)
PREPARATION TIME .... **5 MINUTES**
COOKING TIME .... **2 MINUTES**

200g (7oz) cavolo nero or Tuscan kale, leaves
  roughly chopped, any coarse stems removed
2 garlic cloves, roughly chopped
a handful of basil leaves
50g (1¾oz) blanched hazelnuts (filberts) or walnuts,
  toasted until golden
about 100ml (3½fl oz) extra virgin olive oil, plus
  extra to cover
30g (1oz) vegetarian parmesan-style cheese,
  finely grated
juice of 1 small lemon
salt and freshly ground black pepper

Blanch the kale in plenty of boiling, salted water for a couple of minutes. Refresh under cold water and drain thoroughly.

Blitz the kale in a small processor with the garlic, basil, hazelnuts or walnuts and a good glug of olive oil. Use the pulse button to create a textured paste, trickling the olive oil in until the motor runs freely. Stir in the cheese and lemon juice and season with salt and pepper.

To store the pesto, spoon into a jar, level the top and cover with a thin layer of olive oil, followed by the jar lid. It will keep in the fridge for a week or so.

Sauces

Vegan Nuoc Cham

A vegan-friendly version of the infinitely useful and delicious Vietnamese *nuoc cham*. Vegan 'fish' sauce is widely available in supermarkets these days. It isn't quite the same as the fish-based one – which has extra virgin olive oil-esque tiers of quality and complexity – but it will do nicely for this sauce. Use the *nuoc cham* as a dip or salad dressing, wherever a light touch and a hit of salty-sweet-sour-hot is called for.

VEGAN
MAKES ABOUT 120ML (4FL OZ)
PREPARATION TIME .... **5 MINUTES**
COOKING TIME .... **5 MINUTES**

2 tbsp golden caster (superfine) sugar
3 tbsp rice wine vinegar
3 tbsp vegan 'fish' sauce
juice of 1 large lime

TO FINISH, ADD ONE OR A COMBINATION OF THE FOLLOWING

a thumb of fresh ginger root, peeled and very
   finely chopped
1 fat garlic clove, very finely chopped
2 fresh lime leaves, very finely sliced
1–2 bird's eye chillis, very finely chopped

To make the dipping sauce, gently heat the caster sugar with the vinegar, vegan 'fish' sauce and 4 tablespoons of water until the sugar dissolves. Do not allow the mixture to boil. Let cool. Add the lime juice and whichever finishing aromatics or chilli the recipe requires (you can add all of them, of course, if you wish). Cover and chill for up to 3 days.

Salsa Verde

This is a piquant, mint-heavy version of salsa verde, so you might want to experiment and replace half the mint below with flat-leaf parsley, if you prefer.

VEGAN
MAKES ABOUT 175ML (6FL OZ)
SERVES 4 .... **AS A SAUCE**
PREPARATION TIME .... **20 MINUTES**

2 garlic cloves, roughly chopped
2 tsp Dijon mustard
1 large handful of mint, leaves only
1 small bunch of chives, roughly chopped
1 tbsp capers, drained
2 tbsp stoned green olives
2 tbsp red wine vinegar
5 tbsp extra virgin olive oil, plus extra to serve
salt and freshly ground black pepper

Blitz the garlic, mustard, mint and chives together in a mini food processor until roughly blended. Add the capers, olives, vinegar and olive oil, along with a good grinding of black pepper and 2 tablespoons of water. Use the pulse button to blitz the mixture together to make a textured dressing; it shouldn't be too smooth. Check the seasoning, cover and chill for up to 5 days.

A

B

C

Index

D

E

F

Index

G

H

K

L

M

N

O

P

Q

Index

R

S

T

Index

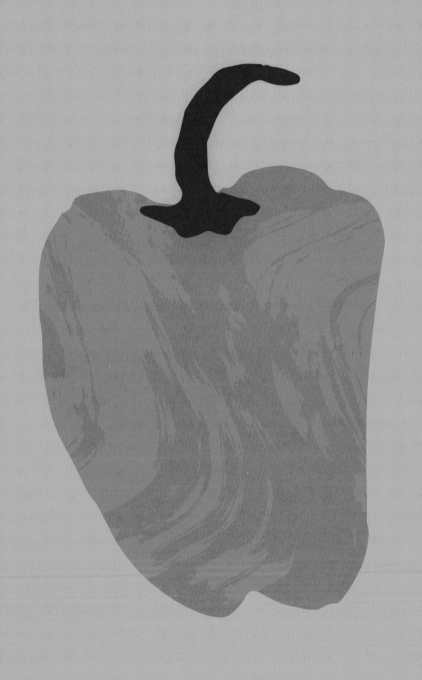

As always, no thank yous would be complete without first acknowledging that any cookery book is a team endeavour. The transition from rough idea to finished article is an enormous leap and not one an author can complete alone.

Thank you to Kate Pollard at Welbeck for her enthusiasm, vision, expertise and friendship. I can't wait to write more of these together. Evi.O-Studio brought these pages to life with colour and imagination – thank you so much! Thanks too to Beth Bishop, Matt Tomlinson, Wendy Hobson and the rest of the Welbeck team for your work on the copy and recipes, making sure everything is clear and shipshape. Thanks Claudia Young at Greene and Heaton for ongoing support and guidance.

Emma Lee, who captured these beautiful, colourful images, is a talent and a dear friend. Emma, thank you for your studio, hard work and all the laughs, as ever. Thank you to Indi and Lily on team photography. Hattie Arnold and El Kemp, we're so grateful for your tireless work and smiles, helping me to cook so many recipes on set. Tabitha Hawkins, on top of your usual star turn with props and Zumba, you brought brownies on a Friday.

About Alice Hart

Alice Hart is an established and experienced UK-based food writer, food stylist, chef, cookbook author and qualified nutritionist (MSc). Her vibrant, seasonal vegetarian recipes celebrate wholefoods, spices and herbs by the handful, as well as vegetables themselves. Alice has written many books to date, but this is her third vegetarian cookbook.